A BRIEF HISTORY
— OF —
BALDWIN COUNTY
ALABAMA

Written and Compiled by
L. J. Newcomb Comings
and
Martha M. Albers
President and Secretary of Baldwin County (Alabama) Historical Society

HERITAGE BOOKS
2025

HERITAGE BOOKS
AN IMPRINT OF HERITAGE BOOKS, INC.

Books, CDs, and more—Worldwide

For our listing of thousands of titles see our website at
www.HeritageBooks.com

A Facsimile Reprint
Published 2025 by
HERITAGE BOOKS, INC.
Publishing Division
5810 Ruatan Street
Berwyn Heights, MD 20740

Copyright © 1928 Baldwin County Historical Society

— Publisher's Notice —
In reprints such as this, it is often not possible to remove blemishes from the original. We feel the contents of this book warrant its reissue despite these blemishes and hope you will agree and read it with pleasure.

International Standard Book Number
Paperbound: 978-0-7884-2604-9

Contents

	Page
Foreword	9
Introduction .... Hon. Peter A. Brannon	11
Baldwin County Historical Society .... Martha M. Albers	13

HISTORY OF BALDWIN COUNTY:

SUBJECT HEADINGS

Five Governments	19
First White Man in Baldwin County	19
Early Indians and Spanish Explorers	19
Indian Villages	21
Indian Mounds	21
Shell Banks	22
Code of Alabama—1923	24
William Bartram	24
From Legend to History	24
Under France	24
From French through British and Spanish Dominion to the United States	25
Baldwin County Created	25
Area and Boundaries	26
Early White Settlers	26
Marchand	27
Interesting Items	28
Nunez Ferry .... Esther Banning	30
William Weatherford—The Red Eagle—Fort Mims	31
From the MS. of S. C. Jenkins	32
"Holy Ground"	34
Fort Mims Monument	35
Animal Instinct	37
Blakeley	37
Josiah Blakeley	45
Fort Blakeley and Spanish Fort	45
An Incident of the War	46
A Relic of the Creek War	48
A Relic of the War Between the States	48
"The Village"	49
D'Olive Cemetery	50
Jackson's Oak	50

CONTENTS—Continued

	Page
Other Points of Interest	50
"Confederate Rest"	51
Alabama Day	51
The Value of an Historic Past............Hon. David Holt	52
Navy Cove............Hon. David Holt	55
Fort Morgan	59
Some Historical Facts about Tensaw........Dr. H. H. Holmes	61
Education	63
The School of Organic Education	64
Revolutionary War	64
Veterans of the War Between the States	65
Veterans of the Spanish War............C. C. Hand	65
Veterans of the Great War	66
The Foley Post No. 99, American Legion........Garrett Foley	68
Civilian War Work	68
Colonies:	
The Italian Settlement at Daphne..........Mary Guarisco	69
Fairhope Single Tax Colony............E. B. Gaston	71
The Friends............Mary Heath Lee	74
Scandinavians at Silverhill..........Dr. O. F. E. Winberg	75
Germans at Elberta............L. Lindoerfer	78
Polish	79
Greek	79
Bohemian............A. F. Wesley and A. J. Cejka	79
French............Carl Boseck	81
Croatians at Dyas............Mrs. Blaz Grdjan	82
Amish............A. N. Schrock	83
Modern Baldwin	84

Introduction

This volume, embodying the results of the efforts of these two zealous officers of the Baldwin County Historical Society, strives to present in a brief way some facts which it is hoped will be the inspiration to those seeking to know that history better to go deeper and to find out more of the traditions of this, one of the most romantic and picturesque sections of the state.

I feel honored in being asked to write a statement intended to introduce it to that public for which it is intended. The eastern shore of Mobile Bay, Blakeley Island, the Tensas country, is Alabama's oldest and at the same time a truly characteristic pioneer section.

The Baldwin County Historical Society has conceived well in its efforts to have the world remember the deeds of those who came, lived and have passed on. This little corner of the state has seen the Spaniard, the Frenchman, the Britisher strive for a foothold and fail. Here America's own nation, the Choctaw-speaking Indians, and America's own white born have been the only ones who have succeeded. They have builded strong. The Choctaws have gone on; those whom we term Americans, in this section of Alabama—amalgamations of romantic Spain, vivacious France, shrewd Scotch, conservative English, mixed yet further with the blue blood of Virginia and the Carolinas—have produced many of Alabama's staunchest citizens. In recent years that influx from the Northern and Western states has caused the revival of the commercial prosperity second to none in the state.

While this compilation claims no final word on the several topics treated, I am happy that I have been allowed the privilege of a small part in the work of this organization and in this presentation of its results.

PETER A. BRANNON

Montgomery, Ala., December 14, 1927.

Baldwin County Historical Society

Object: Preservation of places of Historical Interest and the collection of Historical Data.

It has been said that "there is properly no History, only Biography," and truly it is impossible to record the origin of the Baldwin County Historical Society without referring to the character of the president and founder, Lydia J. Newcomb Comings. Endowed with an inherent appreciation of the scenes hallowed by the trials of the men and women of old, and spurred by the comments of visitors to this section who bemoaned the neglected state of shrines that should be reverently cherished, this noble woman, being one of those "strong souls" who "live to spend their strength in furthest-reaching action," with characteristic energy planned an organization that should have for its object that stated above.

A stormy Sunday afternoon, April 8th, 1923, found a few kindred spirits gathered in Co-operative Hall, Fairhope. Because of the unfavorable weather there was no representation from the other towns of the county, so only a tentative organization was formed, with Mrs. Comings and Capt. John Bowen serving temporarily as president and secretary-treasurer.

But Mrs. Comings' desire to establish a Historical Society had found a responsive echo in many hearts of Baldwin County, and on June 21st, at the Christian Church, Fairhope, there assembled a representative group to organize permanently. The Hon. Peter A. Brannon, curator of the Department of Archives and History, Montgomery, was the distinguished orator upon this occasion, and he inspired an audience that filled the edifice as he eloquently touched upon legend and history that are inseparably a part of our country. With the adoption of a constitution and the election of the following officers the Baldwin County Historical Society was successfully launched and is recorded as the first county organization of the kind in the state: L. J. N. Comings, president; Capt. John Bowen, honorary secretary; William McIntosh, treasurer; Martha M. Albers, secretary—all of Fairhope; Frank Earle, Blacksher, vice-president; additional members of the Executive Committee: Mrs. J. R. Hammett, Daphne; Mrs. O. E. Zundels, Point Clear; Judge W. D. Stapleton, Bay Minette. At a subsequent meeting of this committee A. F. Hutchings, Battles, was designated to fill the place of Mrs. Zundels, who was unable to serve. At every election since organization the membership have signified their approval of the work of those named above by returning them to office. Articles of Incorporation were signed, September 12th, 1923.

The following persons are charter members of the Society; Mrs. L. J. N. Comings, Mrs. M. Rathbone, Mrs. L. J. Bahls, John Bowen,

Mrs. E. L. Gordon, Mrs. Mary H. Lee, T. P. Lyons, Mrs. B. E. Harwood, C. L. Coleman, E. B. Gaston, H. V. Peters, J. R. Cross, Mrs. Mary K. Chapin, Mrs. Cravath, G. R. Cleveland, J. A. Prout, Mrs. Frances Prout, Mrs. J. B. McCall, A. M. Troyer, Elva D. Troyer, O. F. E. Winberg, Mrs. Martha M. Albers, Wm. McIntosh—all of Fairhope; J. R. Hammett, Joe Pose, H. H. Holmes of Daphne; H. Hall, G. W. Humphries, Charles Hall, Mrs. T. W. Gilmer, George T. Byrne, R. B. Vail, W. C. Beebe, W. D. Stapleton, George C. Marlette, S. M. Tharp, of Bay Minette; Mrs. George A. Robinson, George A. Robinson, Mrs. O. Byrne, John G. Aiken and Mrs. J. H. Hastie—all of Stockton; Miss Emily Vail, Mrs. W. A. Stoddard and Mrs. A. A. Rich, of Foley; Frank Earle and Mrs. Frank Earle of Blacksher; Mrs. Gantt, Little River; O. E. Zundel, Mrs. O. E. Zundel and Miss C. Brodbeck, of Point Clear; A. F. Hutchings, Battles Wharf; Mrs. H. M. Lawrence, Dyas; James A. Carney, Carney; W. J. Armstrong and E. G. Rickarby, Mobile; Mrs. Gertrude Murdough, Chicago, Illinois; and Charles H. Brown, Vineyard Haven, Mass.

The Constitution provides that the Annual Meetings shall be held in October, before the 15th of the month, and no effort has been spared to make these notable occasions. Because of the great distances to be traversed in getting from one point to another in the county it has become customary to have these meetings take the form of picnics. October 10th, 1923, was marked by the assembling of nearly two hundred people, representing all sections of Baldwin, at the site of the vanished city of Blakeley. The county Kiwanians met with the Historical Society at this time. There, under the immemorial oaks near Washington Spring, gifted speakers commemorated the valor of those who had founded a "city in the wilderness." Mr. Brannon was again present, and others on the program were S. C. Jenkins of Bay Minette and David Holt of Mobile, while Dr. George C. Marlette of Bay Minette made an impromptu talk. Mr. Holt related the story of another obliterated community in his paper on Navy Cove, which appears elsewhere in this volume.

October 15th, 1924, drew the friends and members of the Society to Jackson's Oak. In this environment, hallowed by memories of the great general and statesman, Frank Stone of Bay Minette, whose erudite mind abounded in historic lore, sketched for the audience the memorable events of the locality.

The 1925 meeting was held on October 8th under the picturesque oaks that border the Bay at Bon Secour. In a scholarly paper that evinced vast and patient research, Samuel C. Jenkins of Bay Minette traced the fortunes of the section through the vicissitudes of four hundred years of recorded history. The occasion was marked by the attendance of the pupils of the Swift Consolidated School located nearby, and many students from the Organic School, Fairhope. Probably one hundred and fifty people partook of the sea-food dinner served by the residents of the vicinity.

Because of unavoidable circumstances it was impossible to hold a meeting in the fall of 1926. However, this failed to diminish interest in the work of the Society, and October 13th, 1927, found the Baptist Church, Tensaw, crowded to the doors for the fourth annual assembly of the organization. The old edifice, erected in 1840, is distinguished by a quaint style of architecture, and in the rear, high above the pews, is still seen the slave gallery—a relic of ancient days. This historic building was a fit setting for the brilliant oratory of Lister Hill, Congressman from the Second District, who inspiringly dwelt upon the life of that great American "Thomas Jefferson; author of the Declaration of Independence; author of the Virginia Statute of Religious Freedom, and Founder of the University of Virginia." Jesse M. Smith of Bay Minette also had a place on the program, and the speakers were introduced by Ernest B. Gaston of Fairhope and Frank Earle of Blacksher. The people of Tensaw, with unsurpassed hospitality, entertained at dinner all who were present on this occasion. The bountiful repast was served in the full beauty of the crisp autumn day at tables placed under the trees near the church.

A feature of the celebration was the unveiling of a steel marker on the highway one quarter of a mile east of the church. In a dedicatory address Mr. Earle stated that the sign is placed on land belonging to one of the oldest Masonic lodges in the state, holding a continuous charter since its organization on December 7, 1855. The marker relates the history of the road in the following legend:

> Indian Trail, Creek Path, 1805. Federal Road, 1811.
> Here was Fort Montgomery, erected 1814 by Lieut.-Colonel Benton of Andrew Jackson's Army.
> Along this way passed Tristan de Luna, 1560; William Bartram, 1776; Lorenzo Dow, 1803; Vice-President Aaron Burr (under arrest), 1807; and over this route traveled the stagecoach in early days.
> Early post office, Montgomery Hill.
> Two miles west was Fort Mims, 1813.
> ¼ mile east, Baptist Church, built in 1840.

Perhaps the most distinguished function sponsored by the Historical Society was the dinner in celebration of Alabama's 106th birthday on December 14th, 1925. In the spacious dining-room of the Beach Hotel, Battles, rich in historic associations, gathered fifty-nine of Baldwin's prominent citizens, representing every quarter of the county. Red and white, the colors of the Alabama flag, were featured in the decorations of flowers and candles, and a handsome birthday cake graced the speaker's table. William McIntosh, as toastmaster, called upon the following, who ably responded: Judge Charles Hall, Jesse M. Smith, G. W. Humphries, all of Bay Minette; Mrs. T. L. Hurlburt, Point Clear; Mrs. Marietta

Johnson, Fairhope; T. J. Dumas, Foley; A. F. Hutchings of the Beach Hotel and Frank Earle, Blacksher. David Holt of Mobile again favored the Society and read a paper of great literary charm on "The Value of an Historic Past," which is given elsewhere in full.

Since incorporation the Executive Committee have made every effort to secure sites of historic interest that are the rightful heritage of the race. Grantors are protected by a clause in the Articles which states that in event of the dissolution of the Society all property deeded to it shall pass into the ownership of the state. From Mr. Earle has been accepted one-quarter of an acre of his estate, Montpelier, containing the graves of Margaret and David Tate and Colonel Tunstall. An iron pipe and cable fencing have been provided for these. The grave of William Weatherford is in the custody of the Society and has been fittingly marked.

The first place to receive the care of the organization was the neglected cemetery at Blakeley. In 1923, under the supervision of Capt. N. L. Durant, this desolate site was cleared of all undergrowth and fallen trees, and later the broken tomb-stones were repaired. Adequate signs directing to Blakeley were placed on the road from Stapleton. The plot surrounding Jackson's Oak was cleared and the stately tree has twice been professionally inspected by order of the Society.

A cherished goal has been the establishment of a Museum, for it is believed that many collections in the county will be gladly given into the custody of the Historical Society when a permanent building has been erected. Various relics have been received from time to time, and early in 1925 a glass case containing them was placed in the Fairhope Library, this building having been designated temporary headquarters. The case contains a number of relics of the Civil and Spanish-American wars presented by A. F. Hutchings, and several books, papers and old letters of historical value were given by R. B. Vail, Dr. and Mrs. Bayard Holmes, P. A. Parker, J. F. Smart and S. C. Jenkins. There is also a copy of a map made of this section in 1615. The original was discovered in the British Museum by Peter Joseph Hamilton, of Mobile, who had three duplicates made. This reproduction was given to the Society by Frank S. Stone, of Bay Minette, who received it many years ago from Mr. Hamilton.

At no time have there been more than ninety-three members enrolled in the Historical Society, although the nominal fee makes it possible for all. Three classes of membership are provided for in the constitution— Active, Sustaining and Life. The annual Active membership assessment is one dollar, while the annual dues of Sustaining members are fixed at five dollars. Any one paying one hundred dollars becomes a Life member. All may participate equally in the control of the affairs of the Society, but Sustaining and Life members have the privilege of designating the purpose for which their fees shall be used.

In carrying out the program of the Historical Society, Mrs. Comings has been ably assisted by Mr. Earle and Judge Stapleton, men whose

A BRIEF HISTORY OF BALDWIN COUNTY

names have for years been associated with every constructive local movement. The work in Tensaw was accomplished against great odds under the supervision of Mr. Earle. The erection of the Weatherford monument meant patient effort in transporting cumbersome material over miles of winding trails followed with difficulty through the dense forest. Judge Stapleton provided laborers and personally superintended the restoration of the shattered stones in Blakeley cemetery.

Since the founding of the organization the need for a simple and easily accessible hand-book of Baldwin County history has been evident and it is hoped that this volume will meet that need. As it is planned that the marker recently unveiled at Tensaw shall be the first of many to be placed in the county, it is predicted that this publication shall be followed by others of similar purport. Those most actively interested, who see so much to be accomplished, are diverted by manifold duties and progress seems slow. But it is hoped that the future will be fruitful of achievement and bring the consummation of the wish lately expressed by Lister Hill—that "the Society shall grow through the years, stronger as time goes on."

MARTHA M. ALBERS

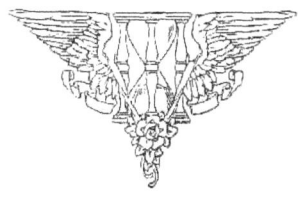

History of Baldwin County

"Matthew Arnold, gifted, cultivated, his mind stored full of the vast history of the old world, while visiting America several years ago, lamented our seeming lack of relics, of antiquities, of castles redolent of historic associations, of towers of old romance; this eloquent paper* shows that one little corner of Alabama, observed by sharp, sympathetic, searching eyes, is teeming with objects, articles and curios connected with its history. The experiences, the incidents, the emotions, the things done and imagined of young countries are quite as full of interest as those of old; they are simply not as many."—C. A. Lanier.

Surely no county in Alabama is richer in historical legend and story than Baldwin. Like the larger territory of which it is a part, it has in its varied fortunes been under the dominion of

FIVE GOVERNMENTS

Spain, 1519–1670.
France, 1670–1763.
England, 1763–1780.
Spain, 1780–1813.
United States, 1813–
Confederacy, 1861–1865.

FIRST WHITE MAN IN BALDWIN COUNTY

It is a matter of record that the first spot in this county to be trodden by the foot of a white man is at a point near Perdido Beach in the southeastern part of the county. A member of a Spanish expedition went ashore there and was captured by the Indians, who kept him with them for a number of years, until finally he was killed at Piachi, higher up on the river Tombecbe. Whether this is legend or history is undetermined.

EARLY INDIANS AND SPANISH EXPLORERS

As early as 1519 the territory about Mobile Bay, called by the Indians Bay of Ochus or Achusee, had attracted the attention of Spanish explorers.

Ponce de Leon had explored Florida, seeking the Fountain of Eternal Youth, and had reported that the Indians found there were most perfect physically and claimed to have acquired their unusual size and splendid physique by drinking from certain springs whose healing qualities cured

---

* "Relics and Antiquities"—paper read by Mrs. Idyl King Sorsby at the annual meeting of the Alabama Historical Society held at Tuscaloosa, June 19, 1899.

or prevented all physical ills which afflict mankind. Tuskaloosa, the Indian chief, is said to have been so tall that when mounted on one of the largest pack-horses of the Spaniards his feet nearly reached the ground.

In 1540 De Soto left his ships in Tampa and marched into the interior in search of gold and pearls, devastating the country, killing and making slaves of the Indians, often keeping prisoner the chief of one tribe until ready to give battle to the next.

But if De Soto and the early explorers were cruel and warlike on their march through the country, the Indians retaliated with bow and arrow and tomahawk. Their approach was so stealthy, their ability to hide so uncanny and their use of bow and arrow so skillful, they proved a constant menace; while in covering any appreciable distance they marched in single file, the last man obliterating all traces of their footsteps, so the white man gained no idea of their numbers.

Later explorers, while never losing their greed for gold or treasure, cared more for colonization and for civilizing the Indians. They were accompanied by numbers of priests whom the Indians came to love and respect, and every Catholic mission was surrounded by Indian families who were taught gardening and other industries.

At the time of De Soto's march through the country, Tuskaloosa was chief of the most powerful tribe in the region at that time, the Mobilians, and also ruled neighboring tribes. With his tried and trusty warriors he engaged in a fierce battle with De Soto, only to be defeated as other chiefs had been before him—and doubtless killed, as he was never heard of again.

This battle occurred at a point claimed by some writers in Greene County and by others in what is now Clarke County. Those of his followers who survived moved further down the river and were found by the French in 1700 near the site of Mobile, and for them (Mauvillians, or Mobilians) the city was named.

About Mobile and Pensacola Bays the Indian population was not large, but the tribes of the interior came to the coast in great numbers at the fish and oyster season.

The Choctaws, Chickasaws and Creeks seem to have been branches of a tribe called Muscogees. The Chickasaws were the fiercest of these tribes, and while the smallest they were the most feared. The Choctaws were a large tribe and were in constant conflict with the Creeks. They lived on or near rivers that empty into Mobile Bay.

In 1715, when the Tensaws were driven out of Louisiana by the Chickasaws, they were established by the French on the Eastern Shore. Many of them became the servants of the colonists who had located here in 1702 and later. Many of these Indians married negro slaves who had been brought to this section in 1699, and some of their descendants are found in the county today. Others, calling themselves Creoles, claim to be the descendants of the Indians and whites who married negroes from the West Indies. Even after the importation of slaves was prohibited, in 1808, negroes were smuggled into the county about Perdido Bay and kept there until they could be sold into the interior.

The French and Indians were always on most friendly terms, and parties of settlers from Mobile—sometimes for lack of supplies at the colony and sometimes for other reasons—were sent to the villages of the hospitable Indians. We have an account of one party entertained by the Indians on the coast and of another by the Indians on Fish River.

In Spanish accounts Mobile Bay is sometimes called Ochus, sometimes Ichuse (or Ychuse), and again Chuse; while on Spanish maps as early as 1520 it appears as Santo Spirito. But since De Soto's time it has commonly been known as Mobile Bay, and has always been one of the important harbors on the Gulf Coast.

INDIAN VILLAGES

The Indians in this section lived in villages surrounded by high walls with numerous port-holes, and in some cases a ditch or moat outside of this. The houses were built of wood—some of them, it is said, being large enough to hold one thousand people. The abodes were arranged around a large artificial mound on which were placed the dwellings of the chiefs. Most of the tribes had attained some skill in agriculture as well as in warfare. Other mounds are found, evidently of more ancient origin, with no trace of having been the site of dwellings.

Aside from mounds, Indians have left few permanent evidences of their presence. As the last warrior concealed their tracks through the forest, so the next civilization destroyed all trace of the Red Man.

INDIAN MOUNDS

Historians differ as to the use of these mounds, some regarding them as burial places, others simply as piles of refuse, while still others feel sure they were used as a place of safety against the encroachment of heavy storms; but most of them agree they were built by the Indians even though their use may be obscure. Also some see in them evidence of a much older (or prehistoric) race. Possibly all are right, and different mounds were built by different peoples for different purposes. If those in Baldwin County could be opened and explored by the proper authorities, it might throw much light on what now seems to be speculation.

At one time permission was asked to explore Knoll Park in Fairhope, on the ground that it might be of ancient origin and contain valuable relics, but nothing was done about it. Some of the finest mounds in existence are within the confines of this county, and the great number of them would indicate that the builders were permanently settled in every part of the county. A few of the smaller ones have been opened and partially explored. Chas. Burkel, of Bay Minette, being much interested in such investigation, has accumulated a most instructive and interesting collection of relics found in some of these mounds. It is hoped that some day these may be in possession of the Baldwin County Historical Society, treasured equally by all who love our county.

Above Stockton, at Bottle Creek, on an island in the delta, is a mound 50 feet high, probably the largest in the county. It is a marvel of industry, made of earth that must have been brought from the mainland in canoes. Some skeletons were found here, but indications are that they were of a later race, as they were near the top of the mound and nails were found in the graves, showing the bodies had been buried in coffins. Possibly they represented some of the early settlers who had fled here for safety at a more recent time.

About eight miles from Stockton is another mound, 40 feet high, 40 feet wide and 100 feet long, on McMillan lands. In a mound near Blakeley was found a burned clay head of much artistic value. At Hall Springs are three most beautiful mounds in a group. On Simpson's Island, at the mouth of the Mobile River, was found a beautiful checkered and engraved bowl turned over the head of a skeleton, and here were unearthed twenty-nine other skeletons. In the mound at Stark's Bluff, on the Bay, were found implements of stone, decorated pipes of earthenware, and a decorated pattern of a stamp in shape something like a bevel, or square. In the mound at Fish River was discovered a vessel with a carved human head of perfect design and workmanship. Perforated discs, which were evidently used in some Indian game, were also brought to light. Similar discs have been found in Canada and Central America. The natives of San Salvador still play a game with discs called "Rooster," or "Little Pigeon." Feathers are stuck through the discs and they are thrown in the air. The game is to see how long they can be made to float there.

In a cave near an ancient destroyed village, Bienville found five clay figures that were worshipped by the Mobilians. They were of a man, woman, child, bear and owl. Whether this was in Baldwin County is uncertain, but some historians locate it at Bottle Creek, near Stockton. The figures were later sent to France.

Two mounds were found near Perdido Bay: one at Josephine post-office containing fragments of pottery; the other at the extremity of Bear Point Peninsula, in which human bones and a number of earthen pots were found.

SHELL BANKS

The shell banks are also of great interest. A short distance south of the old site of Blakeley, along the water front, is a shell deposit of a number of acres. Fragments of ornamental earthenware and skeletons have been found there. The shell banks near Bon Secour, Gasque and other places in the southern part of the county are filled with pottery,

A BRIEF HISTORY OF BALDWIN COUNTY 23

arrow-heads and other interesting things. The surface is now used for truck gardening, and the very finest vegetables are raised there.

On the Brown place, near Bon Secour, is a wall 9 inches thick, made of oyster shells and lime, inclosing a space about 15 feet x 20 feet. Fifty years ago this wall is known to have been at least 5 feet high, but it is gradually wearing away under the storm and stress of varying weather conditions, and is now only 1½ feet to 2 feet high. In one corner of the inclosure is a large oak tree, of an age variously estimated up to five hundred years. Geo. Brown, who lived on this place one hundred and fifteen years ago, records it as an immense spreading tree at that time. After all these years the use to which this inclosure was put can only be a matter of conjecture.

The following is taken from a letter from Herbert Quick, written a few years before his death:

"Some twenty miles south of Fairhope lies a remarkable sandy peninsula, upon which are situated some very interesting places. There is a commodious wharf where steamers may land at Palmetto Beach, and about a mile south is the open gulf with its surf constantly rolling upon a beach as white and smooth as any in the world. Scattered along this coast for a mile or two are some remarkable banks of oyster shells similar to those found elsewhere on the coast of Florida and Alabama. On Strong's Bayou, very close to the Palmetto Beach Wharf, is a very wonderful accumulation of these oyster shells, in which are found fragments of Indian pottery and sometimes human bones. This pile of shells is perhaps twenty-five feet deep. It is an ancient 'kitchen midden,' and was formed about the homes of some ancient people who lived upon shell-fish. Many thousands of people must have lived at Strong's Bayou for generations, eating the oysters and throwing the shells away until they lived upon a hill actually formed from their own kitchen refuse. In this pile some of their dead were buried, and their mingled bones and broken pottery are still found.

"Great trees were found on the tops of these shells, in age probably antedating white settlement. Other shell mounds are made of the remains of clams instead of oysters. Just who the people were we do not know, but to the student of mankind these remains scattered along the coast of Mobile Bay are very interesting, and a visit to the Shell Banks is well worth the time of any traveler."

Many curious relics, pottery, beads, implements and arrowheads have been found at Fly Creek, three miles from the Bay. This creek was called by the Spaniards Volanta, meaning Flying Water, and this name is retained by the little hamlet situated on the bank of the creek. We quote the following from the

CODE OF ALABAMA—1923: *

"The State of Alabama reserves to itself the exclusive right and privilege of exploring, excavating or surveying through its authorized officers, agents or employees all aboriginal and other antiquities, mounds, earth-works, ancient or historical forts and burial sites within the State of Alabama, subject to the rights of the owner of the land, upon which such antiquities are situated, for agricultural, domestic or industrial purposes, and the ownership of the state is hereby expressly declared in any and all objects whatsoever which may be found or located thereon. Sept. 29, 1915."

WILLIAM BARTRAM

It is of interest to note that in 1775 William Bartram, the famous naturalist, made an extended trip through this section including the Baldwin shore of Mobile Bay, devoting much time to the study of plants; and specimens of many kinds of vegetation new to him were sent to England and may be seen to-day in Fothergill's Gardens in London.

FROM LEGEND TO HISTORY

It is impossible in this early history to define localities exactly or to give exact dates, but we now seem to have passed entirely out of the realm of legend and unrecorded events to that of certainty and undisputed facts. Until about 1670 the Spanish were supreme, marching under their yellow and red banners signifying gold and blood, and claiming all the vast territory west of the Atlantic and north of the Gulf of Mexico, as Florida at first and later as New Spain.

UNDER FRANCE

Early in the 18th century the French, having discovered the Mississippi River from the north, attempted settlements along the Gulf Coast, later entering Mobile Bay and finally building Fort Louis on the river at what is now known as Twenty Seven Mile Bluff. After a time (in 1711) this fort was moved to the present site of Mobile. The French claimed a large territory, calling it Louisiana. The Spaniards at Pensacola protested, but in vain, and the French gained a strong foothold on the new continent.

In 1702 the French and Spaniards agreed upon the Perdido River, which is now the eastern boundary of Baldwin County, as the boundary line between Florida and Louisiana.

---

* Sec. 1418. Aboriginal mounds, etc. Right of state to explore, excavate and survey.

When Mobile was founded and the French found themselves in undisputed possession, Iberville planned to win the Indians to the French cause, establish trade with the French settlements in Canada by way of the Mississippi, and so form a great French Empire while keeping the Spaniards in Pensacola and its vicinity and the English to the north along the Atlantic Coast.

FROM FRENCH THROUGH BRITISH AND SPANISH DOMINION TO THE UNITED STATES

On February 10, 1763, by the Treaty of Paris, Mobile and all of West Florida became British territory, and New Orleans and Louisiana west of the Mississippi River was ceded to Spain. The relations between the British and Spanish Colonies were never very cordial, and each made plans to conquer the other at the first opportunity. This chance came when Spain declared war on England in 1779, and a young Spanish Governor named Galvez landed in the bay and bombarded Mobile, finally capturing it.

Reinforcements came for the British, but too late, and the Spaniards met and defeated them on the Eastern Shore and built what was later known as Spanish Fort. After Pensacola had also been captured by the Spaniards the British ceded West Florida to Spain. "The flag with the castle and the lion had returned, and it meant a firmer hold and more lasting rule than in the time of De Soto."

By the Treaty of Paris Great Britain had recognized the independence of the United States, and now it became important to define the boundary line between the United States and Spanish Florida. After some dispute the line of 31° was agreed upon. Some difficulty was found in establishing the line, but in 1813 Mobile and the adjacent country became a part of the United States. "While it was not then realized, this was the beginning of the Spanish retreat before the Americans which has lasted to this day."

Later in this year President Jefferson negotiated the Louisiana Purchase from the French. They received the province from Spain and put up the French flag. A few days later the French turned it over to the United States, and the Americans raised the "Stars and Stripes" over the Cabildo (government building) in New Orleans in token of their supremacy.

The importance of this to this section lay in the fact that the United States insisted that Spain in 1800 had ceded to France and France in 1803 had ceded to the United States all territory east of the Perdido River; hence Baldwin County and Mobile were included. The wording of the treaty was not clear, and the Spaniards did not acknowledge this claim until 1813, when the United States came into full possession of this region.

BALDWIN COUNTY CREATED

Baldwin County was created by the Mississippi Territorial Legislature, December 21st, 1809. It was the third county formed in the State, being taken from Washington County and included much that is now Clarke County. It was still further enlarged by the Alabama Territorial Legislature, February 7th, 1818. Again it was enlarged by the first State Legislature, December 13th, 1819, and again December 16th, 1820, when all that part of Mobile County lying east of Mobile Bay was added, but at the same time all that part of the county west of the Tombigbee and Mobile Rivers was added to Mobile County and that part lying in the fork of the Alabama and Tombigbee Rivers was added to Monroe County. In 1832 the northern boundary was definitely fixed, and in 1868 its area was still further reduced by forming Escambia County from the northeast part. In spite of so much having been taken from as well as added to its original boundaries, it still remains the largest county in the state.

AREA AND BOUNDARIES

The county is 72 miles long and 32 miles wide. It contains 1585 square miles, or 1,014,400 acres. It is bounded on the north by Clarke and Monroe Counties, separated from them by Little River; on the east by Escambia County, Alabama, and Escambia County, Florida—separated from them by the Perdido River and bay; on the west by Clarke, Washington and Mobile Counties—separated by Alabama River and Mobile Bay—and on the south by the Gulf of Mexico.

It was named for Abraham Baldwin, a distinguished citizen of Georgia, in deference to the wishes of the early settlers, many of whom came from that state. He was born in Connecticut, but moved to Georgia when only twenty-eight and represented Georgia in the Convention that framed the Federal Constitution, and from 1789 to the time of his death in 1807 also represented Georgia in Congress. He was the founder of the University of Georgia.

The first county seat was located at McIntosh Bluff, on the Tombigbee. In 1820 it was transferred to Blakeley, and by the same act of the legislature the county court of Mobile was directed to sell the court-house at McIntosh Bluff and divide the proceeds among Mobile, Monroe and Baldwin Counties. A commission was also appointed to purchase a site and erect a court-house at Blakeley, at a cost not to exceed $2,000. The county seat was moved to Daphne by an act approved in 1868, and to its present site in Bay Minette by an act approved in 1901. The first court in Daphne was held under the oaks in front of the Dryer hotel, while they waited for a court-house to be built.

EARLY WHITE SETTLERS

Most of the land grants in this section date from the Spanish period 1781-1813, but some in Baldwin go back to the British period preceding this; and it was during this time that Tories, driven from Georgia, South Carolina and other English Colonies, became the first white settlers and were the ancestors of the half-breeds who afterward played so important a part in the history of the county. The names Marchand, McGillivray, Weatherford, Tate and others became very familiar.

MARCHAND

was a Frenchman. He was in command of Fort Toulouse when the soldiers mutinied, and he was killed. He had married an Indian Princess of the Creek Tribe of the Wind, and had one daughter—Sehoy Marchand. Her first husband was an Indian chieftain, and their daughter was also named Sehoy. She married John Tate, and their children were David Tate and his sister Elouise, who married George Tunstall. David Tate and his wife and George Tunstall are buried in a secluded spot on the plantation of Mr. Frank Earle, in Blacksher. Their graves are marked with marble head-stones in a fine state of preservation. This quarter acre has recently been deeded to the County Historical Society by Mr. Earle and fenced by them.

After Tate's death Sehoy Tate married Charles Weatherford, and two of their children were William Weatherford (Red Eagle) and Betsy, who married Sam Moniac (or Manac).

Mr. Frank Earle's estate is called Montpelier, and it has the further distinction of having been the site of General Andrew Jackson's camp as he passed through Baldwin County in 1814. It was here that he resigned as Governor of Florida in 1821.

The second husband of Sehoy Marchand was Lachlan McGillivray, and their children were Alexander, Sophia and Jeanette. McGillivray was a very successful Indian trader, and when his son was about fourteen years of age he was sent to Charleston to be educated. He remained there sixteen years, when at the age of thirty he in 1776 returned to his Indian tribe and was at once made Grand Chieftain, or, as he termed himself, Emperor. Soon after his sister Jeanette married Le Clerc Mitford, who at once became intimately associated with McGillivray. Mitford was a soldier. McGillivray was a scholar and statesman, whose main effort was to educate and civilize his people; but he realized the need of a strong military leader in case of war, and at his request Mitford was made the Great Warrior.

Their efforts to remain neutral during the Revolutionary War were partially successful, and in 1790 Washington sent for McGillivray to come to him in New York to negotiate a treaty with the Indians. This was finally accomplished, and he was made the Indian Agent for the United States with the rank of Brigadier General. But while McGillivray was away some of the restless Creeks conceived the idea of destroying the white settlements on the Tensaw. His sister Sophia, now Mrs. Durant, learned of this plot at her home near Little River, rode sixty miles on horseback with a trusty negress to call a Council of Chiefs at Hickory Ground Council House. She spoke the Indian language much more fluently than her brother, and had often addressed the Council for him. In response to her pleading, pledges came from all sides of the assembly that the ringleaders should be seized and the enterprise crushed, which was done. It was a heroic act, for two weeks after she had saved the lives of so many human beings she added two more lives, a boy and a girl, to the long roll of the living.

The following Genealogical Chart has been furnished by a direct descendant of Sehoy and Marchand, who vouches for its correctness:

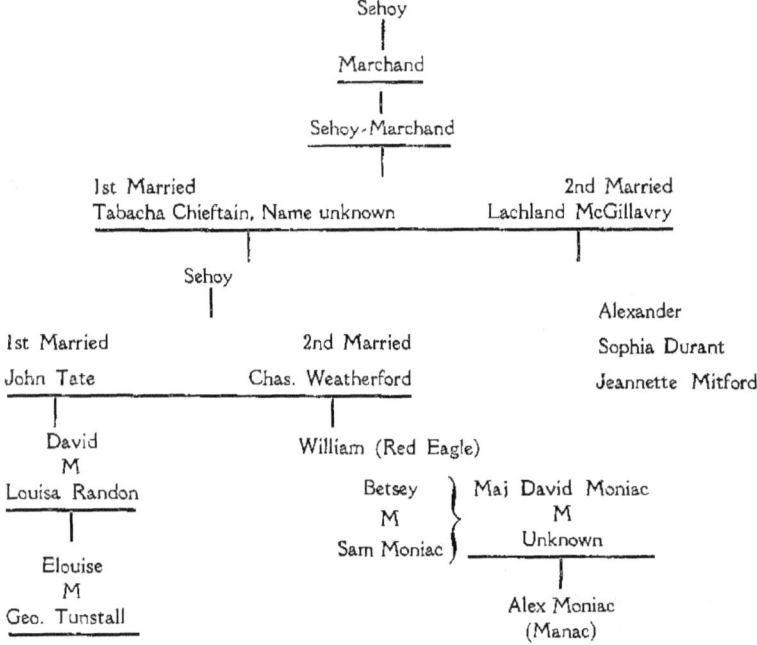

INTERESTING ITEMS

Among these early settlers were many Scotch traders who established regular trade routes and brought in rice, tar and other things which they exchanged with the Indians for hides, skins and pelts. One of the traders, Robert Grierson, raised cotton on his plantation further north in Alabama as early as 1795, and at this time the fertile lands all along the Tensaw and Alabama Rivers were under cultivation by the French people.

From the very earliest historic times, this section of the state has been renowned for its possibilities as a pasturage for sheep and cattle. Prior to 1790, Alexander McGillivray, the native American diplomat, maintained a great "Cowpens Plantation," adjoining Little River; and his thousands of cattle, the hides from which he shipped to Europe, formed a commerce through the Pantons (merchants at Pensacola) which this section of the state has not even yet surpassed.

However, it was William and John Pierce, two brothers from Connecticut, who built one of the first cotton gins in the state. They lived at Tensaw, or the Boat Yard, as it was then called. They had this cotton gin brought on pack-horses from Augusta, Ga., and they set it up for the benefit of their neighbors who were raising cotton. Here the Pierce brothers also built a sawmill and a store, and lived on the shore of what was then known as Boat Yard Lake. In 1709 John Pierce taught the first public school in Alabama, near his home, and William Weatherford was among his pupils.

A map of Mobile Bay made in 1771 by the British Admiralty shows two settlements on the Eastern Shore between what is now Point Clear and Montrose: Weggs, near the site of Fairhope, and Croftown, at the mouth of Fly Creek; and a short distance further north a place called Durnford was owned by the Governor of Mobile. On earlier maps the Eastern Shore hereabouts is called Ecor Rouge, meaning "Red Cliffs." The Red Cliffs were soon recognized as the healthiest place on the Bay, and the Governor of Mobile in 1770 recommended that a suburb of Mobile be built near Rock Creek. Nothing was done, however, except to build a summer resort, and here sick soldiers were brought in relays. This is the place called Croftown, and the people made their own pottery as the Indians had done before and the people are doing now.

From 1805 to 1814 Baron de Feriet cultivated a large tract of land where Fairhope is now located. From Fairhope north extends a bluff for many miles, said to be the highest elevation of land on tide water between New Jersey (some say Maine) and Texas. The highest point is at Sea Cliff, with an elevation of 268 feet above sea level.

In December, 1804, Lorenzo Dow, the itinerant Methodist preacher, passed through the Cut-Off on his way from Mississippi to Georgia, remaining six days in Tensaw. He was the first minister to hold camp meetings and the first Protestant minister in Baldwin County.

Aaron Burr, after his unfortunate duel with Alexander Hamilton, became an outcast from New York. When he completed his term as Vice-President he turned to the southwest, but was arrested for treason in Washington, Miss. He escaped from there and was rearrested near Wakefield, in Washington County, in February, 1807. He was taken to Fort Stoddart, where he was detained two weeks, then rowed up the Alabama River to Lake Tensaw Boat Yard, whence he was taken on horseback under guard through Georgia and then to Richmond, Va.

The first boat to ascend the river from Mobile was "The Mobile," in May, 1819, which went as far as Demopolis on the Tombigbee. The next boat to ascend the Tombigbee was "The Harriot," but it was not until 1821 that this vessel ascended the Alabama, reaching Montgomery in ten days from Mobile, then taking a pleasure party higher up. It is said the first steamer on the Tensaw was so topheavy that a huge cypress log was attached to each side, and they made four miles an hour to Mobile.

In the early thirties an attempt was made to found Alabama City on the present site of Fairhope. A large tract was subdivided and lots sold on the spot and at Mobile and New Orleans. A roadway was cut through the bluff down to the water, and instead of dredging a channel in, a levee was filled out to deep water. A large sum of money was spent in this enterprise, but the panic of 1837 put an end to it. The company was in existence until the War between the States.

In 1820 a stage-coach connected Blakeley and Montgomery, and from there continued to Milledgeville, Ga. Ferries were maintained between Blakeley, Fort Mims and Nunnahubba Island and Mobile— the only means of reaching Mobile from the Eastern Shore for many years.

NUNEZ FERRY—By Esther Banning

Nunez Ferry was started in 1815 by Henry Allen Nunez, who helped build a road from Pensacola to Blakeley in order that there might be a stage-coach route between the two cities. In the early days before the railroad came to this part of Alabama, the stage-coach routes were the quickest means of travel. Stages were run regularly between Pensacola and Blakeley, leaving one city at 6 a. m. and reaching the other at 6 p. m.— a run of twelve hours, which, considering the distance of about sixty miles and the primitive condition of the roads, was making very good time. From Blakeley boats were used to reach Mobile. There were post-houses about every six miles, where four and six horse teams were kept in readiness, and as soon as the stage reached one of these houses a fresh team was waiting. Live Oak Springs, a few miles west of the ferry, was the site of one of these post-houses; also the old Robinson place at Rosinton, the Stapleton (Dewey) place near Loxley, and the William P. Hall place between Loxley and Stapleton.

Nunez was a member of the Florida Legislature in 1840, and in 1849 he received the land on which the ferry had already been located for many years by United States grant under Zachary Taylor. In 1861 he was seized by a band of raiders, who understood that he had a large sum of money hidden on his land. In those days banks were few and far between, and I suppose he often had fairly large sums of money. These raiders tried to make him tell where his money was hidden by hanging him to the branch of an oak tree, still standing at the ferry site, and his wife finally showed them where it was buried under a rose-bush. He was cut down and revived, but did not live very long after his terrible experience.

Nunez Ferry was operated for one hundred and four years, until Sage Bridge was opened in 1919. It carried most of the early travel between Mobile and Pensacola, and for many years the farmers in the central part of the county had no other way to take their produce to market in Pensacola. It is one of the old landmarks of the eastern side of the county, and the new Perdido Bridge on the Spanish Trail is to carry on the tradition binding the old and new methods of travel by bearing the name of the old ferry. The Alabama Highway Department as well as the Florida Department has accepted the name as official.

I could not find any records of the ferry in Pensacola or Bay Minette; but, from the abstract of the property on which it was located, from people in Pensacola who have made a study of the history of Escambia County, and from the stories that some of the people here have heard their fathers and grandfathers tell of the early days of the county, I think it is authentic.

It is also of interest that a trail used by Andrew Jackson called the Three Notch Road crossed the county, touching the present Old Spanish Trail in several places. I do not know the terminals of this road, but one of our neighbors, whose uncle was in Jackson's army, told me that when he was a boy he often saw the blaze (one long scar crossed by three notches) on some of the old trees between here and Nunez Ferry. I think likely the road ran from his camp to Pensacola. There is also a Three Notch Road Street in Andalusia, named from Jackson's blaze.

WILLIAM WEATHERFORD—THE RED EAGLE—FORT MIMS

In sight of Boat Yard Lake stood the house of Samuel Mims, who had made his entry in the British Province as early as 1778. It was around his house that a stockade was built during the Creek War and called Fort Mims.

To understand Weatherford's character one must remember his dual heredity from his educated, disciplined father and his untrained, impulsive mother. Then, too, he was a nephew of Alexander McGillivray, who, though eager for the civilization of his Indian people, was unscrupulous and greedy where his own interests were concerned. He spent much time during his boyhood and youth with his uncle, whom he greatly admired. From him and the Spaniards with whom they associated, he imbibed a deep hatred of the Anglo-Saxon.

He was also a great pet as a boy among the Indians, and at an early age was proclaimed a great leader. He was a fine orator, handsome, brave, athletic, and the feeling of the Indians for him was little short of idolatry. While he possessed many virtues he added many of the worst vices, but that only endeared him the more to his followers. We quote Meek's description of him at this time from "The Red Eagle":

> " * * * * young, eloquent and bold,
> Loved by the young, and honored by the old.
> His word in council, like a trumpet rang—
> Aye, first in pastime or in war he sprang—
> No arm could swiftlier speed the light canoe,
> Or wield the red club with a deadlier blow.
> With these rude attributes, his youth combined
> The nobler graces of a cultured mind,

Drawn from the white man's schools; but still his soul
Disdained the flowery fetters of control,
And turned, untamable, once more to trace
The paths and habits of his Ishmael race.
With them their noblest brave he was esteemed,
Their ruling chief in war or council deemed."

When he saw the gradual encroachment upon their domain, which he realized meant ruin to the Indians, his revengeful spirit became uppermost. He was only thirty when Tecumseh, a Shawnee chief, appeared in 1812, inciting the Indians to a war of extermination, and was greatly flattered when named the leader of the tribes of the south; but even then he seems to have hesitated, and he visited his brother Jack and his half-brother David Tate to consult with them.

Convinced that nothing but disaster could follow, he returned determined to refuse this leadership, but it was too late. He found he could not withdraw, and as the war raged he became a most daring and relentless leader. Thus we find him at the time of the attack on Fort Mims. His Indian blood was in the ascendancy, his hatred of the settlers was fanned to a white flame by fancied or real wrongs, and his one desire was to exterminate the whites and save their hunting grounds for his people.

FROM THE MS. OF S. C. JENKINS

"William Weatherford, when he led his army to the attack on Fort Mims, camped for two days or so at the plantation of Zachariah McGirth, which was a little below old Claiborne. Here he captured several negro slaves, from whom he learned the condition of affairs at the Fort and the best time to attack it. While he was halted at this plantation one of the negroes escaped and conveyed the news to the Fort of the approaching Indians under William Weatherford and Peter McQueen. But, the Indians not appearing, the negroes were pronounced liars; later, two negroes, who were out minding beef cattle, came rushing into the Fort one day and reported that they had counted twenty-four painted warriors lurking in the woods nearby. Captain Middleton was sent out with a detachment of horses to explore, and, finding no Indians or signs of Indians, one of the negroes belonging to John Randon was tied up and severely whipped for what Major Beasley, the Commandant of the Fort, pronounced to be a sheer fabrication. The owner of the other negro refused to allow his slave to be whipped, and was ordered by the Commandant to leave the Fort with all his family on the next day. The negro who had been whipped was again sent out to mind beef cattle, and he again saw the Indians; but he fled to Fort Pierce, being afraid to return to Fort Mims.

"One of the stories about the massacre of Fort Mims is that given by Zachariah McGirth, as related by Pickett. About ten o'clock on the day of the dreadful massacre, McGirth entered a boat with two of his negroes and went out of Lake Tensaw into the Alabama, with the view of ascending the river to his plantation, which was situated below Claiborne, for some provisions; reaching the Cut-Off, he heard a heavy discharge of guns at Fort Mims. With pain and anxiety he continued to listen at the Ferry; then running his boat a mile down the river into a small bayou, he resolved to remain there, being finally impressed with the belief that the Indians had attacked the Fort. Late in the evening the firing ceased, and presently he saw clouds of black smoke rise above the forest trees, which was succeeded by flames. Being a bold man, he resolved to go through the swamp to the fatal spot; when he came within a quarter of a mile of the Fort, he placed his two negroes in a concealed place and approached alone.

"All was gloomy and horrible; seeing that the savages had left, he returned for his negroes and a little after twilight cautiously advanced. McGirth stood aghast at the horrible spectacle before him. Bodies lay in piles in the sleep of death, bleeding, scalped and mutilated. His eyes everywhere fell upon half-burned forms. In vain did he and his faithful slaves seek for the bodies of his family, his wife and eight children, who were all in the Fort when he had left it. Pile after pile he turned over, but no discovery could be made, for the features of but few could be recognized. He turned his back upon the bloody place, crossed the swamp to his boat and paddled down the Alabama with a sad and heavy heart.

"McGirth, now alone in the world, became a desperate man, ready to brave all dangers for the sake of revenge. He fought the Indians through the Creek War with all the might and power that was in him, with the dreadful memory of Fort Mims ever in his mind. One day while McGirth was in Mobile a friend approached and told him there were some wretched Indians down at the wharf who wanted to see him. Repairing there, whom should he meet, to his great astonishment, but his wife and eight children! The scene that Pickett gives of the reunion of McGirth with his family is touching and pathetic indeed.

"The explanation is as follows: Many years before the massacre at Fort Mims, a little hungry Indian boy, named Sanota, an orphan, homeless and friendless, stopped at the house of Vicey McGirth, who was the wife of Zachariah McGirth; she was a Creek woman herself, being a halfbreed; she fed and clothed him, and he grew to athletic manhood, but when the war broke out he joined the war party and was in the expedition against Fort Mims. Like the other warriors, he was engaged in hewing and hacking the females to pieces when, toward the close of the massacre, he suddenly came upon Mrs. McGirth and his foster sisters. Recognizing them in the melee and slaughter, he turned and nobly made his broad, savage breast a rampart for their protection. The next day he carried them on horses toward the Coosa under the pretense he had reserved them for his slaves. Arriving at his own home, he sheltered them, hunted for them and protected them from savage brutality.

34   A BRIEF HISTORY OF BALDWIN COUNTY

"One day he told his adopted mother he was going to fight with Jackson at the Horseshoe; that he might get killed, and that she must endeavor to make her way to her friends on the Lower Alabama. The noble Sanota was killed in the battle, and Mrs. McGirth and her children made their way on foot to the deserted McGirth farm below Claiborne, where Major Blue, at the head of a company of horses, discovered them in great distress and misery. He carried them to Mobile, where they met the husband and father. This story illustrates the character of the American Indian, and shows what his loyalty, fidelity, and faithfulness to friends who were real friends meant to him and to them.

"As a race the Indians are fast vanishing beyond the western horizon; we no longer hear their warwhoop, and their council fires have gone out forever; but their names are upon our waters, they linger along our mountains, and 'ye may not wash them out.' "

It was the British who had sent Tecumseh, the great Shawnee chief, after a conference at Detroit, to stir up the Seminoles, Creeks, Choctaws and other Indian tribes in this section. Tecumseh appealed to them with great fervor and oratory and to their spirit of hatred and revenge; there had already been one battle, the Battle of Burnt Corn, in July, 1813, in which the settlers under the command of Colonel James S. Caller, of Baldwin and Washington Counties, were defeated. After the fall of Fort Mims, Weatherford himself crossed the river into Clarke County with some of his followers, for the purpose of attacking Fort Madison; but on personal inspection of its forces and defences, he decided it was too strong for the forces he had with him. After the war, Weatherford admitted having gone through the entire Fort of Fort Madison and inspected all of its defences without being detected. After pillaging the homes and plantations of the settlers and gathering all the crops they had left standing in the fields in the year 1813, Weatherford and his followers retired to their stronghold, called the

"HOLY GROUND"

This was their sacred ground up the river near White Hall, in what is now Lowndes County. The Indian prophets had told their simple followers, in appealing to their hatred of the white men, if they would go out and destroy their settlements and drive them out of the country, that they would be aided by the British who were at war with the Americans and they could not lose; but if the Americans did defeat the British and sent in armies against them, the Indians could then retire to their "Holy Ground" and no army could take them there. However, in December, 1813, General Claiborne, at the head of the Mississippi troops and some friendly Choctaws, attacked and destroyed Weatherford's stronghold at the "Holy Ground." It was here that Weatherford made his famous leap on his gray horse Arrow from a bluff on the Alabama and saved himself from capture by swimming to the opposite shore of the river.

Mr. H. J. Davis, of Tensaw, owns the land on which old Fort Mims stood; his wife is a grand-daughter of Jesse Steadham, who was one of the few survivors of that frightful massacre. The Historical Society hopes to have the privilege very soon of placing a marker on the exact site.

FORT MIMS MONUMENT

An acre of ground near Fort Mims was deeded to the U. S. Daughters of 1812 in 1917, and they have erected a cairn of rough marble with tablet of polished surface bearing this inscription:

> In honor of the
> Men, Women and Children
> Massacred by Creek Indians
> in Brave Defense
> of Fort Mims
> August 30, 1813.
> Erected by U. S. D. 1812 in Ala., A. D. 1917.

To avenge this awful tragedy at Fort Mims came three armies: from Tennessee under General Jackson, from Georgia under Generals Floyd and Pinckney, and from Mississippi under General Claiborne.

After many battles with the Indians came the great heroic struggle at the Horse Shoe Bend, in which of one thousand Indians engaged only two hundred survived. Then came the surrender of Weatherford, with that speech which comes to us as "the dirge-like epilogue of the woeful drama." Meek thus describes him at this time:

> "A kingly figure, high and proud,
> With nature's faultless grace endowed!
> Fearless in port, as if he trod,
> Like Rob Roy, on his Highland sod!
> His face is calm; no lines of fear
> On brow, or lip, or cheek, appear;
>
> And in his eye, so falcon-framed,
> The native fire is all untamed!
> But still a calmness marks his mien,—
> A sadness in that eye is seen,—
> As in some fountain's limpid breast
> You see the mirrored clouds at rest!
> Those lips, so proud, show, by their press,
> The seal of inward wretchedness;
> And, through that heaving breast, is viewed
> A spirit crushed, but not subdued:
> Yet ne'er did nobler brow or form
> Stern manhood awe, or timorous beauty charm!"

Weatherford, having boldly ridden up to General Jackson's tent, was met by the threatening question: "How dare you, sir, ride up to my tent after having murdered the women and children at Fort Mims?" Weatherford replied: "General Jackson, I am not afraid of you. I fear no man, for I am a Creek warrior. I have nothing to request in behalf of myself; you can kill me if you wish. I come to beg you to send for the women and children of the war party who are now starving in the woods. Their fields and cribs have been destroyed by your people, who have driven them to the woods without one ear of corn. I hope you will send out parties to bring them safely here in order that they may be fed. I exerted myself in vain to prevent the massacre of the women and children at Fort Mims. I am now done fighting. The Red Sticks are nearly all killed. If I could fight you any longer I would most heartily do so. Send for the women and children; they never did you any harm. But kill me if the white people want it done." Jackson protected him from the fury of the soldiers. Later he and Jackson became very good friends, he inviting Weatherford to dine with him and upon his departure presenting him with a fine horse. By some historians it is said he spent a year at the Hermitage, Jackson's home.

At the close of the Creek War the Indians ceded to the United States a vast territory out of which afterward was formed the State of Alabama. One of the provisions of the treaty was that a township of land should be given to each of the heads of the Indian families who had been friendly during the war. Thus the Tates and Jack Weatherford with many others were established in their holdings.

After this Weatherford returned to Little River, and his relatives not only restored his former possessions but gave him of theirs. Here he lived highly respected and beloved by his friends and neighbors until his death in 1824. He is buried where he lived, in a lonely and now almost inaccessible spot near the Alabama and Little Rivers. The Historical Society has marked the spot with a cairn of native stone, with a plain tablet of Tennessee marble bearing this inscription:

William Weatherford
"Red Eagle"
1765-1824

A. B. Meek, in his "Romantic Passages in Southwestern History," printed in 1857, says:

"Weatherford continued to reside at his plantation until the spring of 1824. In that year, we find the following notice in a Mobile paper:

"William Weatherford, the celebrated savage warrior, is, at length, vanquished,—the destroyer is conquered,—the hand which so profusely dealt death and desolation among the whites is now paralyzed,—it is motionless. He died at his late residence near Montpelier, in this state, on the 9th of March."

ANIMAL INSTINCT

Riley tells us that animals were peculiarly sensitive to the proximity of lurking Indians. A horse would stop while plowing, raise his head, sniff the air and show other signs of excitement, invariably pointing his ears in the direction of the danger; so with cows when grazing. They would stop and instinctively lift their heads, raise their tails and point their ears toward the intruder. This came to be an infallible sign which the settlers learned never to disregard.

W. H. Hudson, the celebrated field naturalist, relates similar experiences in South America, where a panic and stampede of horses and cattle often "preceded and gave warning of an Indian invasion—the animals smelt the coming enemy. With the wind blowing from the desert country, this stampede would begin a day or even longer before the enemy appeared on the scene, usually in peaceable times when no one dreamt of such a thing. The panic would extend along the frontier line for a distance of thirty to sixty miles, the horses taking the lead and flying in from the outermost estancias, followed by the cattle."

Riley also tells us the babies and small children never cried when in danger. Even though the mother with her babe in her arms might fall as she hastened to a place of safety, the child was perfectly quiet. The ever-present instinct of self-preservation seems to have asserted itself.

BLAKELEY

To realize the full charm of the ruined city of Blakeley, one must visit the old site, linger along the banks of the Tensaw once teeming with commercial activity, walk along Washington Avenue under the magnificent oaks draped with the somber gray moss, as if so to express their sense of loss and desolation, and visit the one ruin left to show where law and justice were administered—now kindly hidden under a covering of vines and brambles as if to make a brave showing amid so much destruction. Nature is prodigal here, as everywhere, and nothing unsightly has been left. It is hard to imagine this lonely, isolated spot as the city of a happy, prosperous people.

To reach Blakeley, if by auto, one must take a long rough ride after leaving the highway, or if by boat, go up the Tensaw River and then have a tedious climb over the gently undulating country to see all the points of interest.

The cemetery is at least a mile from the river, but it can be reached directly by auto. There are not many markers there, only eleven in all, dated in the first half of the 19th century. The spot where the soldiers who fell in the War between the States were buried is unknown. One monument, more pretentious than the others, is a square pedestal surmounted by a simple shaft, all of white marble. The inscription on the east side reads:

> James W. Peters, Esq.
> 3rd son of General Absalom Peters
> died in this place
> Dec. 1st, 1822
> Aged 31 yrs.
> who with his partner
> Russel Stebbins
> emigrated from New York to this
> country in 1816.
> These two with a few other
> enterprising young
> gentlemen from the North
> commenced in the wilderness and founded
> the town of Blakeley in 1817

On the south side we find:

> Horatio S. Butler
> Son of the
> Rev. D. Butler
> of the City of Troy, N. Y. died
> at this place
> August 4th, 1820
> Aged 28 yrs.

> Henry Boyd
> Son of
> Gen. William Boyd
> of the City of New York
> died at this place
> of malignant fever
> Nov. 27th, 1822
> Aged 21 yrs.

On the north side this appears:

> Ira Hempstead
> Son of Isaac Hempstead, Esq.
> of the City of Albany, N. Y.
> died at this place
> July 20th A. D. 1818
> Aged 19 yrs.

> James Stebbins
> 2nd son of Nathan Stebbins
> of Ridgefield Connecticut
> died at this place
> from a fall from a horse
> Nov. 10th A. D. 1818
> Aged 22 yrs.

The following on the west side complete the list:

> Maj. George P. Peters
> of the
> U. S. Army, 2nd son of
> Gen. Absalom Peters
> of New Hampshire
> departed this life at
> Fort Gadsden, E. F.
> when he was in command
> Nov. 28th, 1819
> Aged 30 yrs.

> Mrs. Lorraine Hitchcock Peters
> consort of
> Major George P. Peters
> died at
> Burlington, V. T.
> April 22, 1815
> Aged 25 yrs.

Most of the graves are marked with upright stones, such as are found in every cemetery; but in a few instances the graves are bricked up and the stones marking them lie flat. We copy all, as it helps us to understand something of the tragedy of this unfortunate community:

               Sacred
       to the Memory of
          John Austin
           who died
        Aug. 20, 1836
            AE 45
This stone is erected in
last tribute of grateful
recollection of his many
    virtues by his
     Son-in-law.

             Sacred
      to the memory of
      Daniel McCall
A native of Society Hill, S. C.
   who died at Blakeley
      Nov. 11, 1839
in the 41st year of his age.
Erected as a last tribute
of esteem by his friends
            J. H. Hora
          Henry Hora
         J. M. Newby

       In memory of
    Mrs. Celia Aaron
         wife of
     Samuel Aaron
who died Oct. 19th, 1824
in the 29th year of her age
And their infant died
    the same day
        also
Sophia Aaron died April 7, 1816
——— Aaron died Aug. 3rd, 1819.

Sacred
to
the memory of
Caroline Matilda Wilkins
born January 18th, 1808
died September 27th
1857

Blessed are the pure in
heart for they shall see
God.

In memory of
Lavinia
relict of
Dr. William Stoddard
born at Guilford, Conn.
died
Nov. 28th, 1820
In the 34th year of her age.
One of the first female
residents in the town of
Blakeley

Lavinia's spirit firm and free
Triumphant o'er the last dismay
Bright in its own eternity
Has passed away.

In memory of
Charlotte
wife of
Dr. Israel Stoddard
born at Guilford, Conn.
died
August 10th, 1820
In the 35th year of her age.
She had resided in
Blakeley
three months.

Who needs a teacher to admonish him
That flesh is grass all earthly things are mist
Dr. Israel Stoddard
died in New Orleans
of the yellow fever 1821.

In
Memory of
Frances Arabella
wife of
Francis B. Stockton
who departed this life
August 28th, 1818
Aged 26 years.

Also
her infant
Son
who died August 28th, 1818
Aged 5 days.

Sacred
to the memory of
Mathurin Reingeard
born January the 31st, 1751
Departed this life December
the 4th, 1822.

Sacred
To the memory of his Son
John Louis Ovide Reingeard
born April the 22nd 1814
who departed this life November
the 18th, 1822.

O God of mercy receive these
souls in everlasting happiness and
join to them all those that were dear
to them

In memory of
William Stoddard
born at Watertown
Connecticut
Emigrated to this state 1817
died
December 23, 1818
In the 38th year of his age.

But all that the blast of destruction can blight
And all that can fade in the tomb
Shall spring from the grave of a brother all bright
In beauty immortal to bloom.

Angeline Knight
born March 5, 1823
died July 24, 1841.

There is a voice I shall hear no more
There are tones whose music for me are o'er,
There were eyes that late were lit up for me,
Whose kindly glance was a joy to see.
Alas! for the clod that is resting now
On those slumbering eyes, on that faded brow.

Also
her daughter
Caroline Knight
born February 22 1841
died September 26th 1841

Sweet little human blossom cropt
Even in thy bud of bloom
How freely will thine angel robes
In fleecy whiteness float around the throne.

In 1923 the Baldwin County Historical Society cleared away all brush and fallen trees and restored all broken tombstones in the cemetery, but the hurricane of 1926 laid low many more trees, some of them falling across graves. Recently (in the winter of 1928) the grounds have again been cleared and fenced and the entrance appropriately marked.

As the eastern approach to the Cochrane Bridge, connecting Baldwin and Mobile counties, is but a few miles from Blakeley, it is hoped a better way of reaching there may soon be provided.

A clipping from the Blakeley Sun, reprinted from the St. Stephens Halcyon under date of February 22, 1819, gives the following optimistic account of the town:

"What a wonderful country is ours! How like enchantment towns and villages rise up! Blakeley eighteen months ago was a wilderness of impenetrable woods, and inhabited by the ruthless savage—but now by the happy and undaunted American. Nothing is now seen or heard but the d n of business and the stroke of the axe resounding through the distant woods—buildings raising their heads in almost every quarter of the town, and the constant arrival and departure of vessels present a scene both interesting and beautiful to the contemplative mind and the man of business.

"We find no hesitation in saying that Blakeley, before many years, will be the chief seaport town in the Alabama territory, it being the easiest of access from the sea of any others; vessels drawing from ten to twelve feet of water can get over Dog River bar (which runs from one side of Mobile Bay to the other), and the same wind that brings them over the bar will bring them up the Tensaw to Blakeley." * * *

So we do know that a prosperous city, with factories, hotels, shipping and beautiful homes, existed here for many years. We are told that many of the soldiers who marched through the country were so impressed with Blakeley that after the Battle of New Orleans they returned and became citizens of Baldwin County, quite a number of the soldiers being eastern men. But the deadly mosquito was responsible for its downfall, and malaria and yellow fever destroyed almost the entire population, the few survivors fleeing to other places.

The town was laid out with broad, straight streets named for famous men—Washington, Franklin, Baldwin, et. al.—while the cross streets were named for flowers, trees and shrubs. There were two public squares, one for public buildings and the other for the market. It was incorporated in 1815. From 1818 to 1828 it contained from 3,000 to 4,000 inhabitants, and rivaled Mobile as a commercial center. It had its newspapers, cotton presses, stores, churches and all that counts for prosperity.

After the scourge of yellow fever in 1826, and again in 1828, the depression was great, and this, coupled with the high prices asked for land by speculators, turned the tide of immigration toward Mobile until not one is left to tell of its former prosperity or to mourn its decline. Besides its one avenue of moss-hung oaks, a single pile of bricks marking the site of the courthouse, and its cemetery among the distant stately pines, with a wonderful spring of crystal-clear water flowing from a

Confederate Rest. - Point Clear

Weatherford's Grave   Fort Mims Monument

Blakeley Cemetery

hillside between the two sites, with hollowed logs used as aqueducts still to be seen, nothing remains but a vast unbroken solitude.

"Nothing in Nature is so full of solitude as a spot where man has been and gone again."—"Trader Horn."

Little is known of its founder—

JOSIAH BLAKELEY

He was born in Connecticut and was of an adventurous and enterprising disposition. He arrived in Mobile in 1806, having spent the six years previous in Santiago de Cuba, and in 1810 took the Spanish oath of allegiance. In 1813 he bought this tract of land for the purpose of founding a city to perpetuate his name. Whether the men named on the monument in the cemetery were associated with him in this, or whether he sold his interest to them, we have no record. Blakeley died in 1815, but it is not known where he was buried.

FORT BLAKELEY AND SPANISH FORT

After nearly thirty years of unbroken solitude, Blakeley again comes into prominence as a Confederate stronghold during the War between the States, with its history of that period so interwoven with that of Spanish Fort as to make it impossible to separate them. Spanish Fort, it will be remembered, was built by the Spaniards under Galvez in 1779 and was considered practically impregnable. It was located near the eastern approach to the Cochrane Bridge, but there is little left to identify the spot.

As in 1781 Spanish Fort, then in possession of the Spaniards, was attacked by the English in their unavailing last effort to establish their supremacy in this region, so in 1865, with Fort Blakeley and Mobile, it was the scene of the last desperate and hopeless stand of the Confederates. The Union forces were in possession of the entrance to Mobile Bay and of Pensacola. Farragut and his forces were in the Bay when it was decided to attack Spanish Fort and Fort Blakeley. One line crossed from Dauphine Island in boats and went up Fish River; the other line marched from Pensacola, paralleling the line of the first, but forty miles to the east. Finally uniting, and outnumbering the Confederate forces about ten to one, they continued their march toward Spanish Fort.

After a two weeks' siege, on April 8th, 1865, following a spirited attack in which many of the officers and men were captured, the garrison spiked their guns, and under cover of the night many made their way to Mobile and Blakeley. The next day several field batteries were moved to Blakeley in the rear of the Union forces, but it was useless, and on April 9th, Fort Blakeley after a brave defense surrendered.

46   A BRIEF HISTORY OF BALDWIN COUNTY

Owing to delayed information this battle was fought after Lee had surrendered and peace had been declared. Three lines of Federal earthworks facing the Confederate fortifications can still be seen, as they are in a fine state of preservation considering that they were built so many years ago. Cannon balls, bayonets and other relics of this memorable battle are still sometimes found.

AN INCIDENT OF THE WAR

has been given us by Miss Clara Hall, daughter of the late Judge Charles Hall, who was so alive to all that concerns Baldwin County. We quote from an article entitled "Alabama to Honor General Canby," printed in an Indianapolis paper in 1923. This was copied largely by papers throughout the East:

"Although he has been dead more than fifty years, General Edward B. Canby, an officer of the Union Army, who was killed in 1876 during an Indian uprising in Oregon and later buried in Crown Hill Cemetery here, has not been forgotten by one whom he supplied with food during the Civil War.

"This was learned yesterday in press dispatches from Washington, saying that President Harding has directed the War Department to ascertain the burial place of General Canby in response to a letter from Charles Hall, an elderly attorney of Bay Minette, Alabama, who wrote that he wanted to put a wreath on General Canby's grave.

"A massive monument stands over his grave in Crown Hill. General Canby was previously buried in the lava beds of Oregon, where he was killed by Modoc Indians.

"Mr. Hall wrote the President: 'General Canby was in command of the Federal Army at Fort Blakeley, Alabama. The Confederate soldiers surrendered to him April 9, 1865, and my father and I later went to General Canby for food. He gave us a wagon load. My father's plantation was destroyed by the soldiers and we had no food for the family—my mother and brothers and sisters.

" 'For many years I have wanted to place a wreath on General Canby's grave. I am now in my sixty-ninth year and I want to place a wreath on his grave before I pass away.' "

In his correspondence at this time, Judge Hall gives a fuller account of this raid on their home:

"After the surrender General Canby remained at Blakeley until the 15th of April. On or about the 11th, about twelve o'clock at night, twenty-five or thirty negro Federal soldiers came to my father's house about nine miles above Fort Blakeley, called him out of the room, beat him over the head with their rifles and kicked him about. They then went in my mother's bedroom in which she and the children were, fired off one of their army rifles and made my mother give them a candle.

"They went into the large dwelling house and set fire to it, and the blaze from this set fire to half a dozen cottages nearby. These soldiers destroyed everything we possessed except the wearing apparel we had on.

"The day after we were burned out my father went to the Fort and called on General Canby and stated to him just how the negro soldiers had treated him. General Canby sent for one of his officers, wrote out an order, and gave it to him and instructed him to take a squad of twenty-five soldiers and go among the negro soldiers, and if my father identified the negroes who burned him out and abused him to line them up and shoot them. Father was unable to identify the negroes; hence none of them were shot by reason of General Canby's order.

"This was a written order, and my father showed it to me after I had become a large boy. In some way this order was lost, which I regret very much.

"On the 15th of April, 1865, I was only ten years, seven months and fifteen days old.".

In 1923, having learned through President Harding and the War Department where General Canby is buried, he seems to have been at a loss to know to whom to entrust this mission, and we find the following in a letter to Dr. Jean S. Milner, pastor of a Baptist church in Indianapolis:

"I take your name from the Indianapolis News of May 4th, and, as I know of no one living in your city on whom I can rely, I am writing to you.

"In Alabama the graves of the Union soldiers are decorated on May 30th. I presume it is the same in Indiana. I want to get you on that day to place a wreath of flowers on General Canby's grave. I am enclosing my check to pay for same."

Dr. Milner replied in part:

"I have your most interesting communication of May 7th. I wish I might reach my hand through this letter and grasp yours.

"You will perhaps be interested in knowing that, in picking me to perform this service for you, you have accidentally picked a Southerner. All of my people fought on the Southern side.

"The old scars of war have healed long ago, and we are today one people throughout this great nation. Beautiful acts like this one of yours have drawn the North and South together.

"As a son of the South it will give me peculiar pleasure to place this wreath of flowers for you on the grave of a great Northern soldier, who befriended you and yours amidst the heat and hate and passion of a most tragic period."

A RELIC OF THE CREEK WAR

After the Creek War, Samuel Worcester discovered an abandoned cannon near Jackson's Oak, where General Jackson had camped. One day, passing there with his oxen and log cart, he took the cannon to his home in Tatumville, about a mile below Fairhope. A few years ago it was exhibited at the Silver Hill Fair. It is now in the possession of Samuel Worcester's grandson, Joe Worcester of Volanta, and has recently been removed to his home on Fish River.

A RELIC OF THE WAR BETWEEN THE STATES *

"In the old fort was a reminder of the Civil War—a rusty cannon, the celebrated 'Lady Slocomb,' banked in the battery. This cannon, an 8-inch Columbiad, was 'cast from Alabama iron in the Confederate foundry at Selma,' and did effective work during the siege of Spanish Fort. Later it was selected to crown Mobile's 'Blue and Gray' peace monument, but was never used. Still later the famous relic was purchased by the Washington Artillery, of New Orleans, and was removed to that city. It has been memorialized in the following lines by the late W. S. McNeill, of Mobile, under date of March 11, 1891:

> Deep in the grass that greener grew,
> That once it was stained a crimson hue,
> The old gun lay, 'neath the sun and the dew
>   Like a warrior dead in his mail.
> Prone on the field where war's high tide
> Had stranded it, yet with a voiceless pride
> It guarded the spot where men had died,
>   Who valiantly scorn'd to fail.
> It guarded those trenches that scarred the hill
> Like furrows of tears, and saw them fill
> With waves of jessamine flowers, until
>   The frown of the field was gone;
> And it watched 'til the men who clinched in the fray,
> The brothers in Blue and the brothers in Gray,
> Clasped hands o'er the gun that thundered that day.
>   True sentry—thy vigil is done!' "

---

* "Lady Slocomb." By Mrs. Idyl King Sorsby.

"THE VILLAGE"

Of "The Village," just above Daphne, Dr. H. H. Holmes says:

"As far back as history reaches we have stories of the Indians who roamed the woodlands of what is now Alabama and of their meetings just north of the Daphne of to-day. It was there that the Tensaws, the Alabamas, and later the Choctaws, the Creeks and the Seminoles, were wont to meet and plan, in their respective ages, the relationships of their tribes. It was there that the French in the days of Fort de la Mobile reconnoitered and planned for their overland trips to Fort Toulouse and other mountain fortresses from Quebec to the Gulf. It was there that the astute McGillivray met with the various tribes of South Alabama, as it was then West Florida, and in his multiple capacity served his own 'Creek Confederacy' and the governments of Great Britain, Spain and the infant 'United States.' It was there that the Spanish Cavaliers bivouacked, as they journeyed to Spanish Fort, only a few miles to the north. It was there that Andrew Jackson held his last council, prior to marching upon Pensacola. It was there that a little city with homes of comfort, well laid out streets and lawns, where pioneer settlers dwelt, was built beside the sea a hundred years ago. It was there that Farragut's men landed the troops, to join and re-enforce those who marched overland to capture Spanish Fort and Blakeley just to the north. It was there that yellow fever, more than a hundred years ago, laid waste those happy homes. And it was there that an old city lies obliterated by the passing of the century."

The Spaniards raided the plantation of Louis D'Olive, who lived near "The Village." He had left the place in charge of an overseer and three slaves, one of whom escaped and gave the information to General Jackson, who at once sent a note to the Governor of Pensacola, where the prisoners had been carried, saying: "An eye for an eye, a tooth for a tooth, and a scalp for a scalp," for any injury done to these persons. They were released and returned to Mr. D'Olive.

Another interesting story was told us of one of the D'Olives—this one somewhat elderly and bald headed. He and one of his negroes were captured by the Indians and carried across the county. There, with their hands tied behind them, they were secured to trees. From time to time the Indians seemed puzzled, regarding them curiously between dances and deliberations, finally dropping off to sleep, when Mr. D'Olive succeeded in freeing himself and his slave and they escaped. Why they were not murdered and scalped, as was customary, could only be conjectured; but the prisoners thought possibly a bald head offered little promise of a good scalp, and the color of the negro's skin, so like and yet so unlike their own, perhaps aroused a feeling of sympathy for them or maybe repugnance at the deed.

D'OLIVE CEMETERY

Near here is the old D'Olive cemetery—just a single lot surrounded by a beautiful iron fence. The graves are all marked with well-preserved stones, but two of them are quite unique and different from anything the writer has ever seen—and she has explored many old cemeteries. The graves are bricked up several feet and the stones are placed upright on the top instead of lying flat, as is customary.

Outside the enclosure is a single grave with a stone in perfect condition, showing that here at some time there were doubtless many other graves, from which all marks of identification have been obliterated. Throughout the county are many isolated graves, some with well-preserved stones and others with inscriptions obliterated or blurred. It evidently was customary to bury on one's own plantation, and often these silent reminders are all that is left to tell the story of the early pioneers.

JACKSON'S OAK

Near "The Village," possibly at the exact site, is a wonderful spreading live oak, with a fringe of silvery gray moss, known as Jackson's Oak. Here General Jackson rested or camped with his soldiers on his march from Mobile to Pensacola during the war of 1812-15, addressing his soldiers while standing on a massive limb of this tree. This is not far from the highway just beyond Daphne. The Historical Society has been promised the land around this tree for a park, and hopes soon to secure a deed for the same. Some show a group of trees as "Jackson Oaks," but, whether legend or history, we like to believe we have found the exact spot and the exact tree—and this is corroborated by the "oldest inhabitants" of the neighborhood.

OTHER POINTS OF INTEREST

All along the Eastern Shore may still be found reminders of the War between the States. At Daphne, at the entrance to the old Dryer residence, once a well-known hotel, is a door pierced by a bullet or fragment of shell. At Fairhope, on the grounds of Oswalt Forster, stands what is known as the Post Office Tree, it having been used as a depository for mail during the war.

The Gunnison home at Point Clear was hit by a cannon ball, and the hole has been covered with a brass plate bearing the inscription: "Compliments of Admiral Farragut—1865."

The dining-room at the Beach Hotel at Battles was built of logs by slave labor before the War between the States. It was originally the main part of the house, but when the hotel was remodeled it was moved back and converted into a commodious and attractive dining-room.

Jackson Oak. — Near Daphne

"CONFEDERATE REST"

The Point Clear Hotel, famous for its hospitality and good cheer long before the war, was converted into a hospital for Southern soldiers during the conflict; and about three hundred of these soldiers were laid to rest in the Point Clear Cemetery. A few years ago the Eastern Shore Memorial Association was formed, with Mrs. L. P. Norville of Mobile as president. They have enclosed this spot with a cement coping and marked it "Confederate Rest."

In 1927, on Confederate Memorial Day, April 26, the date of the evacuation of Mobile, "Confederate Rest" was formally dedicated, among others about twenty-five veterans and U. D. C. attending, the program having been arranged by Mr. A. F. Hutchings. To attempt to give the whole program and the names of all the speakers were futile; but one very attractive feature was the placing of a wreath and bouquet of flowers on each concrete post surrounding Confederate Rest by the pupils of the public school. Archdeacon J. F. Plummer made the invocation, and during the dedication a lovely Confederate flag, which had been presented by L. Hammel Dry Goods Co. of Mobile, was raised.

The day was one long to be remembered: The bright spring sunshine; the south wind blowing through the trees, under which had been placed seats; everything draped in bunting, with many flags, both Federal and Confederate, waving in the breeze; flowers of all kinds, including hundreds of Easter lilies, placed throughout the cemetery, showing that those who had loved ones there had been thinking of them.

ALABAMA DAY

Mrs. Idyl King Sorsby, the founder of Alabama Day, is a native of Baldwin County, and her girlhood was spent at Sibley Mills, three miles east of historic Blakeley. As she picked up relics of war days that spoke so eloquently of patriotic love, she often thought: "How sad that Alabama cannot have a birthday party! I love her, and when I grow up I am going to see to it that she does have one!" And this ambition never left her until it was gratified. In 1897 she celebrated by forming a new club; in 1898, with a family party. But the first formal celebration was held in Birmingham in 1899, when Mrs. Sorsby was director of the Department of History of the Women's Club. It was a great success and proved an inspiration to others to celebrate in later years.

Mrs. Sorsby's zeal was untiring, and in 1923 at a regular session of the State Legislature a joint resolution was passed "that the Governor of Alabama shall each and every year hereafter issue an official and executive proclamation for a state-wide and patriotic observance of the 14th of December as 'Alabama Day,' provided it shall not be a legal holiday." As December 14 is also the date of Washington's death, it has become customary at these celebrations in some way to honor his memory.

At a brilliant dinner given by the Baldwin County Historical Society in the historic dining-room of the Beach Hotel at Battles, December 14th, 1925, the following paper was read:

THE VALUE OF AN HISTORIC PAST
By the Hon. David Holt, of Mobile

In dealing with history one must be careful. The "seeing Mobile" taxi drivers point out the stone cross in Bienville Square as the place where Bienville lies buried. They have told this tale so often Mobile is beginning to believe it. We'll find his bones there some day and then perpetuate the myth.

But for this one day, at least, I propose to be accurate as to facts and choice as to language, so you will forgive me if I consult my notes occasionally.

The subject assigned me on the program of today is "The Value of An Historic Past." Some of my friends, perhaps, would be glad to capitalize their own historic past and others of us would be glad to forget ours.

A land without ruins is a land without history. Man needs an historic background for his best development. We are chameleons in character, taking color from our surroundings.

The citizens of Baldwin County have been gathered and brought together from every state in the Union and from every country in Europe; and yet, all who call this their home can claim a share in everything that Baldwin has in the way of history and records of achievement. All are entitled to pride in its past and glory in its future.

Every nation, state, and community builds for itself a distinctive character. History and tradition as well as education, environment and heredity form the groundwork of this group individuality and animate its spirit. Here lies the greatest value of such a work as that which the Baldwin County Historical Society is carrying forward.

To capitalize the historic past by building shrines at holy places to attract the curious and the thoughtless, the tourist and the spender, would be a sacrilege—like displaying the bones of a revered ancestor and charging admission. Such is not included in my estimate of the value of an historic past.

On the other hand, I have never entered the Alamo, where brave men gave their lives in the cause of Liberty, but some voice seemed to whisper to my inner consciousness:

"Put off thy shoes from off thy feet; for the place on which thou standest is holy ground."

Something of the same feeling would enter the mind of the thoughtful and patriotic American crossing Mobile bay for the first time and recalling the heroic scenes that have been enacted upon its waters and along its shores.

I often wonder if we who live within view of its glittering waves sufficiently value its wealth of history. Christopher Columbus had scarcely been in his grave fourteen years when Pineda discovered Mobile Bay and gave it the most sacred name in his vocabulary—the Bay of the Holy Spirit. He must have witnessed such a sunset as we often have beheld, when the clouds of evening were banked in purple splendor like the pictured throne of a reigning deity, with shafts of light flecked with webs of gold across streamers of tender blue radiating from a scarlet sun. He must have seen the evening star appear as a pale, silver ornament in a canopy of blue, pale rose and gold and watched it grow in brilliancy as the reflected sunlight would fade from the sky.

Here he may have witnessed the splendors of Heaven, even as the prophetic soul of the blind John Milton beheld them, and said in his heart, "surely this is a fit earthly abode for the Holy Spirit."

Here twenty-one years later Maldonado anchored his ships and awaited in vain the return of DeSoto, whose restless spirit found rest beside the mighty Mississippi, which he discovered and which became his grave.

Many songs have been written about Mobile Bay, and its story has been ably told in the histories compiled by Judge Peter Joseph Hamilton. But the living romance, beginning before the arrival of the brothers Le Moyne off the shores of Baldwin County in January, 1699, remains to be written. The matter is all there—war, treasure, romance—but who will combine its elements in the Great Historic Novel of Mobile Bay?

Striking characters march through the pages of its history: Bronze Mobilians; "the Paddlers"; Spanish conquestadores, in search of gold; coureurs de bois, more savage than the Indians; soldiers of France, and the casket girls who refused to eat good corn bread; British soldiers, Spanish soldiers and then Wilkinson's pioneers, destined to inherit and rule the bay and the land.

There is no more heroic chapter in American history than that recorded of the Battle of Mobile Bay. We of the South and those of you who were reared in the North can see this fact clearly now that the smoke and fog have cleared away.

Farragut lashed to the rigging. The guns of Fort Morgan and Fort Gaines answering the guns of the Federal fleet.

"Torpedoes ahead!" yells the lookout from aloft.

The line of ships lashed two abreast wavers, while the guns from Fort Morgan sweep the decks.

"Proceed, gentlemen, regardless of the torpedoes!"

No, the rough old Admiral did not say that. He was not addressing the Historical Society at the time. There were no ladies present. The annals of the United States Navy record that he said:

"Damn the Torpedoes—Full Speed Ahead!" and gave modern Mobile its slogan.

The ironclad Tecumseh, striking a torpedo, sinks. Torpedoes scrape the bottoms of wooden ships and fail to explode through defect in the detonating caps. The line of ships moves on until the obstructions are passed and the guns of the fort are silenced.

Then comes the Confederate ram Tennessee, under command of Admiral Buchanan, and engages the entire fleet of fourteen wooden ships and four monitors. No charge of the Light Brigade at Balaklava was more daring.

A Republican congress has minted a coin as a memorial to the valor of the soldiers of the South and has erected monuments commemorating the valor of the soldiers of the North. We, of the united country, know that these honors were fairly earned and are well deserved. Mobile Bay, theatre of the closing scenes in that greatest tragedy of the Nation's history, will always be remembered wherever the names and deeds of heroes are held in reverence.

Between the site of Fort Mims on the north and that of Fort Morgan on the south, Baldwin County contains many spots of historic interest. This is not a land without ruins nor a land without history.

Before Fort Morgan was built on Mobile point, Fort Bowyer had responded to the fire of British men-of-war, and had driven off a fleet of enemy ships, destroying the British warship Hermes, which lighted the bay with her flames. Later the fort had been captured by the British fleet and army, then but recently defeated by Jackson at New Orleans.

In the war between the sections and in the border wars Baldwin County was often the battle ground. At some point near the Eastern Shore the Spaniards under Galvez defeated the British force commanded by General Campbell, who came from Pensacola to relieve Fort Charlotte, which had fallen before the victorious Spaniards.

Where was this battle fought?

Baldwin County has been Mobile's playground for many years, as well as its battle ground. In the French Colonial days a sweet haven of refuge was the Village, near Daphne. The site still is called the Village, and one of these days, in the near future, it will be repopulated and its departed glories will return. Even before the Village was established, soldiers from Fort Louis de la Mobile were quartered in time of famine with the friendly Indians on Fish River. The historian intimates that the gallant Frenchmen made love to the beautiful and romantic Indian maidens of Baldwin —and they doubtless lived happily ever after.

During all these centuries, the history of Mobile and that of Baldwin County have been closely interwoven. The Perdido River was early made the boundary of West Florida, as it is the eastern boundary of Baldwin County. The same changes of government and conditions have affected the regions on both sides of Mobile Bay, except that the preponderance of commerce has clung to the western shore.

One who studies the topography of Baldwin County and observes how its bays and rivers, its ridges and watersheds, extend to points on the coast contiguous to natural deep water, cannot fail to wonder why the original colony and seaport was not on the Eastern Shore, instead of at the mouth of the Mobile River. I predict that there will yet be a great seaport in Baldwin County.

Two mosquitoes, one bearing yellow fever and the other conveying malaria, are responsible for the abandonment of the thriving seaport of Blakeley and the consequent change in the destiny of several generations of Baldwin County citizens. Had Blakeley survived, with its cultured founders from the older centers of American civilization, its shipyards, deeper natural channel and better port facilities, it doubtless would have become a railroad terminus and would have continued a formidable rival to Mobile. Yellow fever and malaria visited Mobile, but a greater proportion of its population was composed of natives, immune to yellow fever and acclimated to malarial conditions.

The first successful steamboat that plied Alabama rivers, the Tensaw, was built at the shipyards of Blakeley, in 1819. An effort to establish a city on the Eastern Shore was made by a company of real estate boomers from New Orleans in the early thirties. Fairhope does not desire a speculative boom. But Alabama City, on the same site, prayed in vain for a boom. Had it arrived it might not have been unmixed evil. It might have led to an earlier improvement in public education in the county and kept young men at home who scattered to the four winds for want of educational and commercial opportunities in their native fields.

Now, after all these years, Baldwin County is coming into its own.

Vandals denuded its hills of their virgin pine with a wasteful carelessness that wrought its own punishment and loss. But now the builders of homes, industries, highways, bridges and railroads are at work and are surveying preparatory to further operations. They will build upon a surer foundation, plant their fields, orchards and vineyards, and rear a noble tribe of Baldwin men and women, true to type, tradition and the ancient landmarks builded by the heroes and pioneers, founders of the county and of our Nation.

Therein lies the true value of an historic past.

At the annual meeting of the Historical Society held at Blakeley, October 6th, 1923, the Hon. David Holt read another interesting paper, which is reproduced herewith in full:

NAVY COVE

It has been my good fortune to visit several of the so-called "dead towns of Alabama," including Cahaba, St. Stevens and Blakeley, and to write something about each of them. I have visited Old Cleborne, on the bank of the Alabama, and have wandered among its graves. There is some spark of life remaining in all these dead towns. Several negro cabins face the streets of the state's first capital, Cahaba; St. Stevens lives again in a nearby village of the same name. At least one of the old residents, with his store, and a score of others dwell upon the site of Cleborne. Blakeley is not without its living inhabitants, and will once more spring into some semblance of life when the Mobile-Baldwin bridge is built to make it more accessible.

But there was one sweet village in Alabama and in Baldwin County that can never live again, except in the tender memories of a few men and women who remain to tell of happy days spent there amid surroundings that were too near the ideal long to endure.

Navy Cove, on September 5, 1906, was a village of fourteen contented homes and a population of about forty persons. Before the end of the following day it was a desolation, and even the ground upon which it stood had been rushed away by storm-driven waves.

"Scenes and Stories of the Storm, September, 1906," a booklet which I published shortly after that harrowing disaster, gives this brief description, under the heading, "Navy Cove Washed Away:"

"Where once the village of Navy Cove overlooked the waters of Mobile Bay, something more than three miles east of Fort Morgan, now nothing remains but a few battered and wrecked houses, for the storm played havoc in the little harbor and six lives were lost there, while many others narrowly escaped.

"Captain Denny Ladnier and his daughters were saved by catching in the branches of a floating tree and were brought ashore after the wind had subsided by a sailor who chanced to see them in the debris of the bay. Mrs. Ladnier and four sons had been drowned and their bodies were washed out to sea. Where the Ladniers' home stood is now a lagoon, with ten feet of water. Where the Smith home stood is now an inlet from the bay with a depth of twenty feet.

"Forty persons were saved at Navy Cove on a knoll east of Mr. James Duggans' residence, where four oak trees stood. When the waters began to encroach upon the land from the Gulf on the south and Mobile Bay on the north nearly all of the inhabitants of the village reached the knoll. Sailors among the party secured ropes and passed them around the oaks, forming a life line, to which the people clung while the waves beat over them.

"The topography of the peninsula where Navy Cove stood has been entirely changed. The sand hills which protected the cove from the wind and waves of the Gulf were blown or washed away, leaving a bare and barren waste, except that here and there some sturdy, windshaken tree stands as a sentinel above the ruin.

"The body of Mr. Johnson, an aged gentleman who was drowned at Navy Cove during the storm, was found and brought to Mobile for burial."

Captain Joseph H. Norville, a former member of the legislature, was reared at Navy Cove, as were several others among the active Mobile Bar pilots. His description of the life at Navy Cove, when he was a boy and young man, and until the time of the storm, brings vision of an existance approaching the ideal; of a condition where neither poverty nor riches were known and a community where all were neighbors in the truest meaning of an often misused word.

There were no locks upon the doors, no bars at the windows. There was no representative of the force and power of the law, for none was needed. St. Andrews Bay, immediately to the east—now on the charts as Andrews Bay to distinguish it from the Florida estuary of the same name—was literally paved with the finest oysters, which could be gathered by hand when the tide was low. Wild ducks, including mallards and canvas backs, came early and remained throughout the winter. Fresh and salt water fishing, the best and most various, could be enjoyed at all seasons.

At night, when the weather was fine, the young people would build fires of driftwood at points along the beach, and there all would congregate to talk and sing; to love and laugh and live.

One mile to the south the Gulf dashed its surf upon a long, smooth beach, the sand hard-packed where wet and flaky and white as snow where it was dry. But boys and girls did not go in swimming together then, as is now the custom.

Each family had its city friends who went to the Cove in summer, and there was interchange of visits between Mobile and the village at all seasons of the year. But, as a rule, the residents of the Cove were sufficient unto themselves for their own company and entertainment. Their wants were few and were abundantly satisfied. The young people owned their boats and sailed where they wished to go. Dances were frequent at the homes and at other points along the Baldwin County shore, and these were attended by sailing parties, all neighbors and friends.

It was the constant association with the water from their earliest youth that made the Navy Cove boys among the most skillful small boat sailors in the world and caused them to follow naturally into the chief business of their fathers and uncles—that of piloting vessels across Mobile Bar into the bay, and to the point where they were taken over by the river pilots in those days, if they were to proceed all the way to Mobile.

The greater part of Mobile's commerce before the war between the sections and for many years thereafter was conducted with lighters which loaded and unloaded ocean-going vessels anchored in the lower bay. In those days the Cove had numerous visitors from many lands. But there was never a hotel or boarding house at the village and there was no thought of commercializing the attractions of the place. It was just home, and that's all.

From memory, Captain Joe Norville gives this list of the residences as they stood upon the peninsula: that of Captain Edward Dorgan, Captain W. T. Norville, Joe's father; E. T. Allen, Dave Coster, John Smith, George Cook, John Ladnier, James Duggan, Andrew Dorgan, William Johnson, H. C. Wilson, Denny Ladnier and Mrs. Walsh; the last named having formerly been the home of Captain Charles Wallace.

The only one of these that remained standing after the storm was the Denny Ladnier home, and it was tilted at two angles from perpendicular, in such a manner as to give one looking out from its doors or windows a most peculiar sensation of unreality and out-of-shapeness. Naturally, the house acquired the reputation of being haunted.

Several years after the storm, Captain Curtis Johnson, Mobile Bar pilot, who loved a practical joke, happened to be at Navy Cove on an occasion when a party of sight-seers were in the act of disembarking to see the far-famed "haunted house." To spread its reputation as such was a powerful temptation to the captain. He found an old dishpan and a brick, climbed the stairs and waited until the visiting party entered the room below. Then Curt turned loose his spirit and there was ghostly rattling up-stairs. The excursionists departed with more haste than dignity—all except a boy and girl, aged about eight and ten.

"We aint 'fraid of ghosts!" yelled the boy.

"Come back here, Johnny!" screamed his mother.

"We'll find the ghost," Curt heard the girl say.

And they did.

"Here's your ghost!" the two children shouted in chorus, and the captain stated on the word of a pilot that he has never felt so totally cheap in his life as when those wise-eyed children saw him seated on the floor with a pan in one hand and a brickbat in the other, impersonating a ghost.

Those of you who have visited the Beach Hotel, at Battles, may have seen in Mr. Hutchings' cabinet of curios a sugar bowl to which the shell of an oyster is attached.

That sugar bowl was on the table in John Ladnier's home at Navy Cove when the storm broke in its fury on the 6th of September, 1906. Three years later, Mr. Ladnier picked up his sugar bowl while tonging for oysters in the bay, three miles from where his home had stood until it was totally destroyed by wind and wave.

Some day, in the cool of the evening, when the wild chase after the things that men pursue ceases to drag me into an unwilling commercial trot, I hope to take up this subject and follow it further. In the meantime, the students of Baldwin County history will at least find a suggestion for their research from this brief sketch of the dead village of Navy Cove.

A Gun Pit

Section of the Fort viewed from across the old moat

Civil War Section of the Fort at left
Spanish-American Section of the Fort at right

Officers' Quarters

SOME VIEWS OF FORT MORGAN

A BRIEF HISTORY OF BALDWIN COUNTY

FORT MORGAN

Compiled from unsigned articles in the "Mobile Register."

Historic old Fort Morgan, abandoned military reservation on Mobile Point, at the entrance to Mobile Bay, has been purchased from the United States Government by the State of Alabama for use by the State Docks Commission in development of the State's seaport at Mobile. With the transfer of Fort Morgan there comes to the State of Alabama all the glamour and glory of what once was the strongest point on the Gulf Coast, and the site that was made famous in one of the greatest naval encounters of all time.

Fortifications have been maintained on old Mobile Point for more than 113 years. Before Fort Morgan was there, Fort Bowyer was built in compliance with an order of April 20, 1813, and named after Major John Bowyer. However, Fort Bowyer was never taken seriously until Andrew Jackson repaired it and garrisoned it just in time to resist the first fierce British attack, on September 15, 1814. The beating which the British took from Fort Morgan kept them away for several months; but on February 11, 1815, just a little over a month after the battle of New Orleans, they swarmed back to Mobile Point with thousands of men and several ships. After one of the fiercest little battles in history, Fort Morgan fell, and the British invested the fortifications. But on April 1 they withdrew.

For several years after the War of 1812, Fort Bowyer lay idle and deserted, or with a skeleton garrison, on Mobile Point. In 1837 it was superseded by Fort Morgan, which was maintained until the opening of the War between the States, when Governor Moore of Alabama ordered it seized, as well as Fort Gaines, for the Confederacy.

It was on August 5, 1864, that the battle of Mobile Bay, in which Fort Morgan played so heroic a part, was fought. Rear Admiral Farragut had been ordered to the Gulf in January, and he decided to attack Mobile and stop the running of the blockades; but it was not until August that he was assured of sufficient naval and land co-operation to assure the success of the attack. At the head of the Federal fleet he steamed toward Mobile. In the way lay only the Confederate ram "Tennessee," aided by three auxiliary gun-boats—puny things at best; and the entrance to the Bay was guarded by the yawning guns of Fort Morgan on the east point and Fort Gaines on the west. All across the entrance, save for a narrow channel under Morgan's guns, piles had been driven and torpedoes laid, so that the entire entrance was effectively blocked—or so the Confederates thought. However, imbued with the spirit of Farragut and his "Damn the torpedoes! Go ahead!" the Federal fleet beat its way into the harbor. It plowed through the torpedoes, which had been thought adequate protection, but which failed to explode even though they could be felt bumping against the ships.

And then came the most gallant episode of the naval history of the war. The "Tennessee," with her guns trained and every man at his post—every man knowing that death was a matter of but a few minutes—steamed out and attacked the entire Federal fleet. It was a futile gesture, but a glorious one, and one that will ring down through the ages as an example of how men die for an ideal. It was short lived. Superior forces won. The Federal forces took Fort Morgan. But they dared not attack Mobile. And so Fort Morgan slipped back again into the hands of the Federal Government, where it has been until to-day, when it once more returns to Alabama, the state whose blood has more than once drenched the 322 acres of its expanse.

The history of Fort Morgan seems to have been one of alternate decline and rehabilitation. After the war it was allowed once more to fall into decay. But when the thunder of military conflict rolled up again on the horizon, and Spain and America collided, there was a logical fear that the great Spanish Armada might steam up into the Gulf, pass in through the blank, blind eyes of the two old forts, and set her foot in Mobile, where once before her flag had flown.

And so, in 1898, Fort Morgan was rehabilitated. New quarters were built, and a new disappearing battery installed, separate from the fortifications, which were armed to the rim and entirely renovated. But Dewey's strategy discouraged the Spaniards at Manila, and again Fort Morgan retrograded to slumber and degeneration.

Then came the World War, when the booming of drums and the clarion call of a world plunged into conflict and turmoil woke the old fort from its sleep in the languorous life of the sub-tropics, on the golden shores of the Gulf. From a garrison of two companies maintained at the fort in 1914, both Gaines and Morgan were designated as concentration points and training camps. Once more the walls re-echoed to the rapid, short steps of marching, to the stirring strains of reveille and the soothing song of taps. Again clean-cut officers barked orders that reverberated from the barracks, and enlisted men toiled day and night to learn the art of killing people.

Then the war was over—sooner than was expected—and Fort Morgan was again abandoned. The old fortification was used to it by this time. It rather welcomed the sleep and the dreamy ennui that had been its lot alternately with stirring battles and booming guns for 114 years. It retrograded genteelly. And so it is to-day—obsolete, useless, abandoned, but covered with glory, steeped in the lore of battle, and echoing the ghostly screams of dying men.

A BRIEF HISTORY OF BALDWIN COUNTY 61

The following paper * was intended to be read at a meeting of the Historical Society at Tensaw, Baldwin County, October 13th, 1927, but was received too late:

SOME HISTORICAL FACTS ABOUT TENSAW

By Dr. Herbert Hilary Holmes.

Whenever the tourist travels in any of the European countries, or in Canada, he is struck by the little country villages, with their neat, well-kept homes clustering about an elegant church edifice. This is especially noticeable in the French sections of the Province of Quebec. I recall pointing out to Mrs. Holmes, on our steamer trip out the St. Lawrence and up the Saguenay Rivers this past June, one such village on the banks of the Saguenay, with but seven homes, and near the center was a handsome church building constructed of the gray granite of that section. This is an evidence of the fact that, in the very beginning, the settlers have erected altars to their God, and adorned their house as evidence of the real faith they take with them everywhere.

America, by which I mean our own United States, has shown no less a faith. In all sections of our country, though, there is not just one elegant church, about which all the wealth of the village is centered, but in most of them there are several buildings. This is in keeping with the fundamental principles as written in the Constitution of the United States. Each citizen is guaranteed the right to worship his God according to the dictates of his own conscience. Insomuch as the Catholics and all the various sects of the Protestants have helped in the making of America, it is but right that they should have had their faiths guaranteed unto them.

Today we welcome you into a village that has seen every phase of American history. Just across the river from Dixie Landing, but a short distance away, is Choctaw Bluff, where was fought the first great battle between the Indians and the whites on any of the soil of what is now the United States. It was in 1540 that DeSoto with his cavalier soldiers besieged the walled city of Mauvila, and after a long and desperate struggle destroyed the strength of that brave warrior, Chief Tuscaloosa, whose fate remains a secret to all posterity. A skeleton unearthed by my father and uncle on the banks of Pine Log Creek, together with the copper buttons and insignia on the casket, was identified as that of a soldier of DeSoto. Near by was an oak tree, felled, perhaps at the same time, which was completely petrified. The lower trunk showed the ax marks of a long past era.

If the battle of Fort Mims were in progress today, as it was on that hot August 30, 1813, when William Weatherford surrounded our ancestors

---

* By Dr. Herbert Hilary Holmes, of New York City. (A communicant of the Montgomery Hill Baptist Church; a former Senator of Baldwin County; a former President of the Daphne State Normal School; now instructor in Psychology in N. Y. Training School for Teachers.)

and after a complete surprise attack butchered, after the most horrible fashion of Indian warfare, those 555 brave souls, no doubt we could hear the fusilade, the wailing of women and children, and the fierce war-whoops of the warriors. Near by that fort was erected by one of the Pierce brothers from Vermont the first cotton gin in the state.

Today we are all proud of the great work that the present legislature has done with regard to the education of the youth of our state. You see just across the road our little school. It has had many predecessors at nearby spots in our village; in fact another of the Pierce brothers taught the first school for whites in all Alabama just under the highlands on the road to Fort Mims. On almost every hill for miles around were built elegant homes by the old settlers, who came to make their fortunes by farming the fertile valleys of the Alabama and Big Bee Rivers. Many of those still stand —monuments to a more prosperous past. Some of these settlers came during the Spanish possession of this territory, now a part of West Florida. The Weekleys, Belts, Booths, Pierces, Steadhams, Holmeses and Moores were among the first settlers of Alabama.

We invite you to see those homes. Look about you. Note the gallery under which you entered here today. That gallery was erected so that the slaves of our ancestors might be led unto salvation by the same divine worship that served as an inspiration to their masters. The home of the masters was the central home of each and all of the slaves. The church home of the masters was the church home of the slaves. The ministers of the masters were the ministers of the slaves. That was the spirit of our ancestors. The long peaceful relationship existing between our white and colored citizens of old Montgomery Hill, as our village was called prior to its being changed to Tensaw, is proof of the long-ago good work of our forebears. We had a common cause and worshipped God in unison.

The present building was begun some thirty years before the War between the States. It had a predecessor here, but its beginnings were laid by that godly soul, Lorenzo Dow, who made his rounds over the entire country and in those rounds always included Fort Mims. Thus we date back in actuality for more than a century. Aside from the custom of many of the older settlers, who buried their loved ones near their homes— such as at our home, the Booth graveyard, and the Weekley burial-ground— and those who buried their dead at Old Turners Hill near Majors creek bridge on the highway, you can read much of our past history from the tombstones about our church. Would that you could visit them all! Not only was this a great meeting-place for friends for more than a century, but I am sure that history will bear out the statement that this present church was the centre of the first prohibition section of Alabama. The legislature of 1870 was petitioned to make it illegal to sell whiskey or other intoxicating drinks at any place within a five-mile radius of this Montgomery Hill Baptist Church. That law has never been repealed.

Insomuch as it would be impossible to trace the records showing all the distinguished ministers who have served this people, I shall not attempt to enumerate them; but by reason of his long and valuable services to us and our people I may say that the Rev. Andrew Jackson Lambert covered 56 years of that history. So deeply was he imbedded in the religious life of this people that no baptism and no marriage was considered binding and no funeral was appropriately conducted unless the rites were performed by "Uncle Jack" Lambert, as he was familiarly known. Until his son, the Rev. J. S. Lambert, was called to Montgomery, by the Department of Education, he ably filled his father's place. Many association meetings were held here. Broadus and many of his contemporaries have heard the echo of their voices from the old gallery under which you entered.

Thus, friends and fellow-citizens—you who come from many sections far removed from dear old Alabama, though many of you have known no other home—we are indeed glad to welcome you into the most fertile section of history in the entire state. Mrs. Comings, we are grateful to you for bringing the Baldwin County Historical Association among us. Study our past. Read the doings of the wonderful years now long gone in the ruins of Fort Mims, at the tomb or grave of Weatherford, about our church and churchyard, and know for a fact that I speak the sentiment of seven generations of loyal Baldwinites when I welcome you here today.

EDUCATION

As has already been stated, the first public school in the county as well as in the state was taught near Tensaw by John Pierce in 1799. For half a century education was in a decidedly chaotic condition, but in 1850 the legislature attempted to bring about a degree of order by putting the schools of each county under the control of its Judge of Probate. As these judges already had more than they could well do, this added duty received little attention, and in 1855 the office of County Superintendent was created by the legislature. Interest was aroused by this act, and there has been a steady growth and improvement. No record can be found of the early County Superintendents in Baldwin. J. S. Lambert served for eighteen years (1900—1918), and his successor, S. M. Tharp, is still in office. There is also a County Board of Education of which the County Superintendent is secretary ex-officio. The steady growth and advancement throughout the county attest their constant and untiring effort to build a school system second to none in the state or nation.

All of the larger towns of Baldwin as well as many of the smaller ones have good brick buildings according to state plans. Foley, Fairhope, Loxley and Robertsdale maintain accredited high schools, while Bay Minette has the County High. The consolidated school system prevails, and the children are transported to and from school at public expense. In the country districts are to be seen many good frame buildings, and usually very near by the community church of varying denominations.

The culmination of the county school system is the Class "A" Normal School at Daphne. It is accommodated in the remodeled buildings formerly used for the Courthouse and Jail.

The negroes of the county are generally self-respecting and law-abiding. They have their own schools and churches, and their schools are under the control of the County Superintendent of Education. They too have a Teachers Training School at Daphne called the Eastern Shore Industrial School, a boarding as well as day school and a part of the public school system.

As an incentive to the study of history, the Woman's Civic Club of Bay Minette is offering prizes this year (1927-28) for the best essay on the history of Alabama by a high school pupil, while Robertsdale is also offering prizes for the best essay on Baldwin County history. So we find Baldwin forging to the front educationally as well as in other ways.

THE SCHOOL OF ORGANIC EDUCATION

at Fairhope has, since it was opened in 1907, always attracted a goodly number of educators and others interested in Progressive Education as visitors, while pupils have come from all parts of this country, and a few from foreign lands have attended the school.

The aim of the school is for greater freedom for the child, less domination from his elders, greater opportunity for initiative and self expression and a complete absence of self consciousness. There are no examinations for "passing", no daily marks to worry both teacher and pupil, no set form to which the child must be moulded, just the ideal to work toward— a controlled, cultured body and mind, and a harmonious spirit. This is not a preparation for life. It is life.

The Six Weeks Winter Course for adults brings together a most congenial company who always seem happy and interested whether listening to Mrs. Johnson's lectures, working in the Arts and Crafts and Manual Training departments, studying Nature's mysteries, exercising in the folk dancing or merely watching the children in their regular work.

REVOLUTIONARY WAR

A short distance from Blakeley, remote from all signs of travel or habitation, at the summit of a long grassy slope heavily shaded by swaying pines through which the sunlight flickers, is Saluda Hill Cemetery—just one enclosed family burial place with a few scattered graves around it, but of immense historic interest, for here lies buried a Revolutionary soldier, the only one so far as known in Baldwin County. The grave is bricked up about two feet, and the stone that marks the spot and is remarkably well preserved bears the following inscription:

Sacred
to the memory of
Zechariah Godbold
a native of
Marion District, S. C.
who departed this life
July 13th, 1832
aged 69 years
3 months and 10 days.

At an early age he joined the
ranks of Genl Marion in that
eventful struggle which was
over Independence.
This stone is erected by his
widow and son in testimony
of their esteem for a kind husband,
indulgent Father and generous friend.

VETERANS OF THE WAR BETWEEN THE STATES

Of the War between the States there are a few Confederate Veterans still living in Baldwin County, and many buried here. As the years have passed, Union soldiers in their declining years have sought homes in this milder climate, and some have "passed out" while here, in many cases finding their final resting place in southern cemeteries. This has been especially true of Fairhope, where heroes of "the blue and the gray" rest in close proximity.

VETERANS OF THE SPANISH WAR

(By C. C. Hand, of Bay Minette)

I appreciate your request for some information regarding Spanish-American War Veterans from Baldwin County, Alabama, since it seems so few realize or appreciate the services rendered or the hardships borne by the Volunteer boys of 1898.

This was a 100% Volunteer army who by their spontaneous response to their country's call broke the morale of the Spanish Army and brought the war to a victorious close almost before it was started, and for the first time in its history made the United States of America a recognized world power. This by an army unsuitably clothed, inadequately armed, and improperly fed, who had needless suffering and death from dysentery, typhoid, yellow fever and malaria, who ate embalmed beef in the various camps and were poisoned by it for life: these are the boys who by their sufferings taught the War Department how to save the boys of 1918 from like disaster.

From these men more than one-half of the field officers of the World War received their training; every Army commander, every corps commander, every division commander and nearly every brigade commander was a Spanish War veteran—to say nothing of General Pershing himself. Yet we seldom see or hear anything said or done in recognition of their services in 1898.

The Spanish-American War began April 21st, 1898, and officially ended April 11th, 1899. The last Alabama Volunteer Regiment was mustered into service at Mobile May 1st, 1898, and discharged October 31st, 1898, at Birmingham. So far as the writer knows, all of Baldwin County men were in the Second Battalion, Company "I", which was from Oxford, Alabama, with the following officers: Captain, A. Harrison; 1st Lieutenant, T. B. Cooper; 2d Lieutenant, Clifton B. Sitton; 1st Sergeant, J. M. Armstrong ("Nervy"), who afterward served as Sheriff of Baldwin County.

The writer recalls only ten men from Baldwin County in the First Alabama regiment—as follows: R. D. McConnell; T. A. Carr; F. M. Thomas; Willard Hamilton; John Jones; J. L. Skipper; Walter Gentry; Wm. H. Horton; our bugler from Daphne, Alabama; J. L. Feminear and C. C. Hand. Regimental officers: E. L. Higdon, Colonel Commanding; D. D. McLeod, Major, Second Battalion; Chaplain, Captain O. P. Fitzsimmons.

VETERANS OF THE GREAT WAR

Baldwin County gave its full quota of soldiers to the Great War, and the list of honored names of those who made the supreme sacrifice is a long one:

THE WORLD WAR HONOR ROLL OF THOSE FROM BALDWIN COUNTY WHO DIED WHILE SERVING IN THE ARMED FORCES OF THE UNITED STATES

Tobe Arnett, Gateswood
Dan Broughton, Hurricane
James H. Bryars, Stockton
Joseph W. Bryars, Perdido
Aurelius M. Carpenter, Carpenter
Little Ed. Durant, Bromley
William L. Gilmore, Fairhope
John R. Givens, Robertsdale
Daniel M. Grimes, Daphne
Edward T. Harris, High Pine
Leroy Knight, Dyas
Willis J. Lassitter, Scranage
Ray E. Lewis, Daphne
Hobson Maddox, Stapleton
Aubrey Mitchell, Lillian
Minter M. Moorer, Bay Minette
Wm. E. Morris, Loxley
Jos. J. Patton, Battles Wharf
Greil Roberts, Bay Minette
John G. Robinson, Daphne
Douglas M. Taylor, Bay Minette
John T. Taylor, Bay Minette
John T. Weeks, Magnolia Springs
Thomas W. White, Robertsdale

COLORED

Boston Brown, Perdido
Raymond Jones, Daphne
Madison Ladd, Tensaw
William Sledge, Bromley
Wilson Williams, Tensaw
Hilliard Wright, Blackshear

THE FOLEY POST NUMBER 99, AMERICAN LEGION

(By Garrett Foley)

"Foley Post No. 99 is the livest post in the State" was the answer of one of the State officers of the Legion to an inquiry as to which post to join. The Post was organized in April, 1925, with one hundred and twenty-five charter members and M. Holm the first commander. In August, 1926, under E. Murray as Post Commander, the Post won a spirited contest with Huntsville for the 1927 convention, being the youngest Post in the State. The 1927 American Legion Convention was held at Foley August 21, 22 and 23, and was the largest State Convention ever held by the Legion. In 1927 the Foley Post was one of three awarded citation from National Headquarters for the greatest gain in membership. At this State Convention E. Murray, Past Post Commander, was elected a State Vice-Commander.

This Post is county wide and takes in all Baldwin County, being one of the largest Posts in the State. In all civic affairs, such as assisting the Boy Scouts, Junior Chamber of Commerce work, and charity, Foley Post takes a leading part and observes Armistice Day each year with appropriate ceremonies. In order to get all citizens to vote, a member of the Post has offered a silk flag to the Post that gets out the greatest percentage of the registered voters.

The present Post Commander, G. Foley, is preparing plans for a home to be built on two lots given to the Post by the Magnolia Springs Land Company. There is a large and very active auxiliary, of which Mrs. W. Dyer is the present efficient president.

CIVILIAN WAR WORK

To mention by name the earnest, faithful war workers would be to enumerate almost the entire population of the county, both men and women. The National Council of Defense, 4-Minute Men, Red Cross—every branch of the work was represented, and all did their best. In every drive, sale of Liberty bonds, or whatever the call, Baldwin went "over the top." Her record may be marked 100%.

COLONIES

In the latter part of the 19th century, and the early part of the 20th, a number of groups of various nationalities and ideals, actuated by different motives but all attracted by the climate, soil and healthfulness of this section, settled in Baldwin County. The first to come were the Italians. A short sketch of each colony follows, either written by a member or prepared from data furnished by one or more.

THE ITALIAN SETTLEMENT AT DAPHNE

(By Mary Guarisco)

This colony had its beginning in 1888, when its founder, Alesandro Mastro-Valerio, came here and bought a tract of government land which he later sold to his colonists. His purpose in organizing this colony was to induce the Italian immigrants of this country to till the soil, thus taking them away from the large American cities. Mr. Mastro-Valerio realized that his countrymen could live a better and richer life in a rural environment than in the packed quarters usually given to immigrants coming to the large cities. The future welfare and progress of his fellow-countrymen, which could be better secured in the agricultural field, was the motive underlying Mr. Mastro-Valerio's action. This venture was not connected with the Italian government.

Mr. Mastro-Valerio gave fourteen years of his life to this colony, educating them in sound principles of rational agriculture. He was then, too, experimenting for the United States Department of Agriculture and the State Experiment Station located at Auburn. He is now in Chicago, where he is editor and manager of La Tribuna Italiana, an Italian newspaper.

It was in 1889 that Mr. Mastro-Valerio came here to stay. During this year the first two Italian families came; namely, Mr. Domenico Trione's family and the Castagnolli brothers. He later brought twenty Italian families and influenced several others to come. He did this by newspaper advertising and by sending circulars throughout the North. The majority of Italian families coming to Daphne were from Illinois. These people did not all come here at the same time; twenty years elapsed between the arrival of the first colonist, Mr. Trione, and the last, Mr. Joseph Drago.

Each colonist possessed from twenty-five to fifty acres of land, bought for from $1.50 to $5.00 an acre. The colonist built his house out of lumber cut from trees felled to clear his land for cultivation. The culture of rice, tobacco, sweet and white potatoes, wheat, cotton and vegetables was going on. They set out vineyards of grapes imported from Italy, and domestic grapes for commercial purposes. Several families were successful in winemaking; however, this has been discontinued. Looking over the products these same farmers now raise, we find potatoes and green corn the leading ones, while the production of rice, tobacco and wheat has been discontinued.

One of the first tests of permanent colonization was signified by the purchase of a plot of ground upon which the colonists built their little church of The Assumption. The church now standing is an enlargement of the former one. These same people are now working for the building of a new church, a larger and better one that will fill the needs of a fast-growing congregation. Last year brought the addition of a rectory for the presiding pastor, which is one of the best of modern homes, not only of this community but also of the nearby communities.

After a favorable report from Professor Guido Rossati, who published a book in Rome on Italian colonies and settlements, Margherita of Savoy, then queen of Italy, sent as a gift some rich and artistic vestments, an illuminated missal, and two boxes of books to this church for the Feast of the Corpus Christi, June 9, 1898. These vestments are still treasured by the church and used only on state occasions. This proved that the Italian colony of Daphne was appreciated by the Italian government, and especially by the queen, who claimed the title of "the elder sister of the Italians, wherever they are, at home or abroad."

One cannot mention the church without recalling the Rev. Angelo Chiariglione, better known as "Father Angelo." He came here in 1897 as the first resident priest of this parish. Since there was no rectory at that time, he had a small study in the home of Mr. C. Bertagnolli, where he lived. He gave the last eleven years of his life to diligent labor for his community, where he was pastor, teacher and friend. His pockets were nearly always empty, for he gave his meagre salary to the poor, especially to children who chanced to need help. It was sad tidings when one morning in September, 1908, Father Angelo was found dead, seated on a log, where perhaps fatigue from walking had compelled him to rest. He was buried in the front churchyard. No minister of the gospel, regardless of creed, has since been respected and honored as has been Father Angelo.

On June 30, 1913, a meeting was called of all the Italians for the purpose of organizing a society or club. This society was called the Progressive Italian Benevolent Society. In 1915 it was registered in the County Record books at Bay Minette. While this society cannot boast of any individual founder, it can claim as its head, from the very beginning, Joseph Drago, who had been its president until October, 1924, when he returned to his Italian home at Palermo after an absence of twenty-five years.

The aims of this society are as follows: To be more progressive through co-operation; to attempt to solve any problem that may arise among themselves; to help any member of this community who needs assistance in any way; to be in harmony with all public institutions. All these aims have been carried out as the need arose. During the World War this society gave one hundred dollars to the Red Cross drive. One hundred dollars was also given to the Daphne Normal Fund. Since the growing prosperity of the Italians here no longer demands as much activity as formerly, the society is not as active; however, there is still a reserve in the treasury for future public benevolence.

This colony can rightfully claim Mr. Frank Manci, who came here in 1897, as its greatest business man, and to him it owes much of its early progress. If cotton raising was to be extensively and successfully carried on, a local gin was a necessity. The nearest cotton gin, at that time, was fifteen miles away, where these farmers took their cotton the first years. In 1900 he put up a cotton gin. A year later he put up the first saw mill.

The first store bore the sign, "Frank Manci, General Merchandise." Other early business men are Messrs. C. Bertagnolli, C. Allegri and Corte. Bertolla and Allegri now have large storehouses for produce at Loxley, where all farm produce from Belforest (the farming section of Daphne) is shipped. These represent the largest growers and shippers not only of the Italians but of the county as well.

Even though this colony has not grown by further colonization, it has grown in other ways. The farms that formerly were from twenty-five to fifty acres are now one hundred and two hundred acres, which likewise shows financial growth. There are 1,600 more or less acres in cultivation every year, making an average of about one hundred and thirty acres to the family. These farmers use scientific methods and the most improved farm implements, which accounts for their achievements. Each family has its truck for farm use, thus making it very convenient for them to keep in touch with every one. In 1920 a Home telephone was put in all the homes at Belforest, proving their appreciation of modern improvements. All the Italians have nice homes fitted up with modern conveniences.

This group of law-abiding Italians, now American citizens, are carrying out the work started by the colony founder, Alesandro Mastro-Valerio, who in recognition of this piece of work has been made a Chevalier by the Italian government.

FAIRHOPE SINGLE TAX COLONY

(By E. B. Gaston)

Among the several "Colonies" whose origin and achievement help to make up the interesting history of Baldwin County, and which have contributed in varying degree to her upbuilding, one differs from all others in being founded neither by a racial group nor for the financial profit of the founders, but around an ethical ideal, in the hope of furthering its wider acceptance by a demonstration of its soundness and beneficence when put to the test of practical application.

The Fairhope Single Tax Colony had its inception in the winter of 1893-94, with a small group at Des Moines, Iowa, whose common convictions and personal friendship brought them frequently together, and who conceived the idea of giving practical test to the teachings of Henry George in a Colony founded upon land which they might secure in some favorable location then unknown.

Single Taxers hold as a "self-evident truth" that all men have equal right to the use of the earth (without which they contend indeed that the assertion of the Declaration of Independence of the equal right to "life, liberty and the pursuit of happiness" is meaningless). They hold that, as a natural result of the coming of people together in communities—local, state or national—and of the activities of governments which they institute for their benefit, land values arise, and that these land values, bearing a direct relation to population and to public needs, are therefore obviously a proper source of public revenue. They hold still further that in any properly organized and administered government the land values would yield sufficient revenue for all proper public purposes, rendering it unnecessary to tax forms of wealth that, instead of being due to the community, are the result of individual industry and thrift—hence the conception of the land value tax as the only (or "single") tax.

The problem of the Single Tax Colony was to apply these ideas of taxation in spite of contrary ideas applied by the government. To accomplish this the Colony makes use of the legal right of individuals or corporations to acquire land and dictate the terms upon which they will permit its use by others—subject, of course, to their right to accept or reject its terms; its terms being that the holders (under long-time leases, the land never being sold) shall agree to the collection of the full annual rental value of the land alone, exclusive of improvements made by the lessees, and the application of the rentals first to the payment of the taxes of all lessees—again regardless of whether their holdings be improved or not—whatever remains to be expended for the common benefit; the lease contracts providing expressly against any portion of the rents being expended as dividends or otherwise for the profit of the Colony corporation or of individuals.

Attention of the Iowa group was first directed to Alabama by a gentleman from South Dakota who had met at a conference of Single Taxers in an eastern city Mr. E. Q. Norton, of Daphne, who proved at that early day to be an excellent "booster for Baldwin." A committee spent over sixty days in investigation of various localities suggested, and its report, made in the Fairhope Courier, publication of which was begun in Des Moines, Iowa, in August, 1894, was the basis of a vote by those interested, which was overwhelmingly in favor of a location on the Eastern Shore of Mobile Bay, though no land was acquired in advance of the coming of the initial group.

The first party of Colonists landed at Battles Wharf, in Baldwin County, on November 15, 1894. It consisted of eighteen adults and nine children. There were seven adults and four children from Iowa, four adults and three children from Minnesota, two adults and two children from Ohio, two adults from Pennsylvania, two from Vancouver, B. C., and one from Missouri. Of the very first party, few had ever seen one another before the assemblage at the "promised land." Of the eighteen adults only nine actually located in the Colony they came to found, two are still living in it, and two are buried in its cemetery.

Several weeks of consideration by the pioneers, the original group being re-enforced by others, was given to the choice of the exact site. The first purchase of some 150 acres, costing about $6 an acre, included a half mile of Bay frontage. Two hundred acres adjoining, distant from the Bay, was bought at about the same time for $1.25 an acre.

The holdings of the Colony have been added to until they now embrace over 4,000 acres. Land alone was assessed for taxes in 1927 at $190,960, improvements swelling the total to over $629,000, with the large building program of 1927 not yet appearing on the assessment. It is doubtful if any equal area in the county, not excluding the county seat, shows as high an assessed valuation.

Figures of rent collections give further excellent proof of the growth of the Colony. Rents collected were only $175 in 1898. Ten years later they had risen to $3,195; in another five years (in 1918) to $8,015; in another five years (in 1923) to $19,234 and in 1926 to $24,777.

Education has ever been one of the major interests of Fairhope people. The only school in the immediate vicinity when the pioneer colonists arrived was one conducted for a few months in the year in a little cabin near the home of John I. Gabel. It was about 12 x 14 feet in size, with wooden shutters in lieu of windows and the rudest kind of seats, and was presided over by a quaint character named J. C. Finklea. The members of the Colony at once took steps to do better for their children, and established its own school, the first teacher of which was Clarence L. Mershon, later very widely and favorably known as Dr. C. L. Mershon, a leading physician of the county.

The expansion of the school facilities was rapid, in keeping with the growth of the community, or in advance thereof. Today Fairhope's educational equipment includes a consolidated public school, with accredited high school, housed in a handsome modern brick building, costing about $20,000, to which at present (December, 1927), in its third year of use, extensive additions are being made, which will when completed nearly double the investment; a grade school conducted in another excellent two-story concrete block building, and the School of Organic Education, founded about 1907 by Mrs. Marietta L. Johnson, assisted by Mr. and Mrs. S. H. Comings, which occupies eight buildings on a ten-acre tract (the use of which is given by the Single Tax Colony). This latter institution has a teaching and administrative force of 20 persons, and has attained not only a national but an international reputation.

Akin to her exceptional educational facilities, Fairhope has a free public library, probably superior to any to be found in any other town of its size in the South. Begun in 1898 by Mrs. Marie Howland, with a nucleus of books accumulated by herself and her husband in New Jersey, and later taken to Topolobampo, Mexico, and then returned to the United States, accretions have been continuous until it now has about 10,000 volumes, housed in an attractive and commodious building. The library is the property of the Single Tax Colony, which in 1924 made extensive additions to the building. It is open daily for the free use of residents and properly sponsored visitors upon payment of a small fee.

The Single Tax Colony has probably made Fairhope the best advertised town on the Alabama coast. Numerous articles have been published regarding it in newspapers and magazines, some of them of very wide circulation, and many students of sociology come to investigate its working at first hand.

Its extraordinarily attractive location, and the wise provision of the founders in reserving practically all of its Bay frontage for public enjoyment, have helped to make it a very popular resort, both in summer and winter.

Fairhope, with an area of approximately 1½ miles square (about half of which is Single Tax Colony land), was incorporated as a municipality in 1908. Upon incorporation the Colony assumed the payment for its lessees of their town taxes, as well as the state and county taxes hitherto paid. The town is second in population and voting strength of the towns of the county and growing at least as fast as any.

THE FRIENDS
(By Mary Heath Lee)

Among the various groups that have made Baldwin County distinctive, and have helped in its development and real progress, are the Friends, or Quakers. Although not a large community, theirs has been one with a positive influence for good.

In 1910 Marion Smith and Franklin Rockwell, with their families, attracted by the Single Tax principles on which Fairhope was established, came down from Kansas. They were followed by others, but probably Iowa has contributed more than any other state, although Ohio, North Carolina and Vermont have furnished their contingents. It is not easy to estimate their number, as it varies from year to year, being augmented each winter by those remaining only during the colder months. There are generally about twenty families living permanently near Fairhope, while as many as forty families have at one time or another made their home there.

The farms are all on Colony land within a radius of five miles, with a meeting house and a school building about two and a half miles from town. Meetings for worship are held twice a week, and the group is under the control of Ohio Yearly Meeting. Visiting ministers come occasionally from Philadelphia and western states, and the meeting is the central force in the community.

A few years after the coming of the first families a school was opened. The attendance varies from fifteen to twenty-five, and two teachers are employed when necessary.

Nearly all the families were experienced farmers in their northern home states, and consequently know how to meet the problems here, which in the beginning were those of pioneering life and conditions. A number of pleasant homes and good farms have resulted from their efforts.

Several members of the community are members also of the Single Tax Corporation, and active in affairs connected with the welfare of the Colony, with others conducting business of various kinds. The farmers, both men and women, are diligent producers of fruits and vegetables and growers of cattle.

True to the principles of Quakerism, the Friends of Fairhope stand for peace and brotherhood.

SCANDINAVIANS AT SILVERHILL

(By Dr. O. F. E. Winberg)

It is said that Silverhill derived its name from a man living on a hill in the vicinity where the village is now located. While the man's name was not Silver, it is said that he did not handle any other money than silver—therefore they called him Silver; hence the village name. However that may be, it is a fact that the name Silverhill appears in the records of the express company as early as 1861, with this notation: "Express office Mobile; Post Office address Daphne." The writer is informed that Silverhill in those days extended from Fish River to Black Water.

Silverhill, as we know it today, was founded in 1897 by Oscar Johnson, C. O. Carlson and C. A. Valentin, of Chicago, Ill. It was the intention of the founders to establish a purely Scandinavian colony in Alabama, and, after investigating the Gulf Coast region thoroughly, these gentlemen decided upon the present location of Silverhill, in Baldwin County. Land was acquired by purchase from a Mr. Harford, the first block of land being 1,500 acres, which was added to from time to time as the colonization work progressed.

Scandinavian settlers came to Silverhill from virtually every state in the Union and began the development of what is now the Silverhill district. They found the soil responsive and the climate ideal, and it soon became known among the Scandinavians throughout the country that Baldwin County in Alabama was, without a doubt, one of the most beautiful spots in the country. As a consequence, people readily responded to advertising, and almost every month, from October to May, large parties of home-seekers came to the newly founded colony. It was pioneering, however, in the fullest sense of the word. There was no railroad from Bay Minette to Foley in those days. Whatever was produced had to be hauled to Marlow and then transported by boat to Mobile, or else hauled to Daphne and from there to Mobile by boat. It was, of course, impractical to load in carlots and ship to northern markets as is now done; consequently, the farmers were dependent upon the Mobile market, which at that time was not sufficient to take care of the production. The result was that while the new settlers were delighted with the climate, the productiveness of the soil, the pure water, etc., what they produced brought them no revenue; and most of the settlers, having no capital to rely upon, had to seek work outside of their farms and many were compelled to return to the North to earn a living. Notwithstanding the hardships incident to pioneer life, however, the colony made progress.

One of the first things that the colony did, under the leadership of Oscar Johnson, was to provide schools. The public school, in the early years of the colony, was conducted in what is now the office of Oscar Johnson. It continued there until 1904, when the present school building was erected. The site for the school and lumber for the building were provided by the colonization company, and the labor was performed by the settlers themselves; thus, what was then a good school house was provided. The county and the state at that time did not provide sufficient funds to carry on the school more than four or five months in the year. The Scandinavian settlers, most of whom were born in Scandinavia, were not satisfied with so short a school term for their children, so they voluntarily agreed to tax themselves per family in order to provide a school term of eight months a year.

The Scandinavian people are religiously inclined, and consequently one of the first things the early settlers did was to build churches. The colonization company assisted by giving sites and lumber from their sawmill. Soon the colony had grown to such an extent that it was possible to have a minister stationed in the community. The first church established was the Baptist, and after that the so-called Mission church, which is an offspring of the Lutheran church. Many of the settlers were Lutherans, so it was not long before the Augustana Synod showed its interest in the community by sending missionaries. Services were held in the school house. In recent years a neat Lutheran church has been built in Silverhill, with the aid of the colonization company, which donated a site for the church as well as otherwise assisting. A permanent minister has been maintained by the Lutheran congregation for many years past.

The settlers early realized the possibilities for dairying, and, not being able to get an income sufficient from the growing of what is commonly known as truck crops and fruit crops, they began to acquire dairy cows and to make butter at home, which was sold wherever a market could be obtained in the county. In 1907, Mr. C. O. Carlson, one of the founders of the colony, induced an experienced dairyman named Claus Frisk, of Wisconsin, to come to Silverhill and look over the field. Mr. Frisk found it promising, and during the year moved to Silverhill and built a creamery, which he conducted until 1920, when it was destroyed by fire. Mr. Frisk shared in the pioneering activities of the community—its successes and disappointments; but he stuck to his undertakings, and through it has added materially to the prosperity of Silverhill, and incidentally his creamery has been the means of dairy development in other sections of the county.

The Bay Minette and Fort Morgan railroad was built in 1905, and opened a new era for Silverhill and the entire southern portion of Baldwin County. In 1906 the farmers of Silverhill, and throughout the county,

A BRIEF HISTORY OF BALDWIN COUNTY 77

began raising crops such as Irish potatoes and cucumbers on a large scale for shipment to northern markets. It was not a success from the start. The farmers started out in 1906 with great hope of profit, but when the season was over they were sadly disappointed because the returns they had been promised did not materialize. They got bills for freight ranging from 50c to as high as $55 for some farmers. This surely was not encouraging, but they were undaunted and went after it again the following year with somewhat better results; and then year after year, until they learned from experience the necessity for co-operation, which finally brought prosperity. Instead of the farmers seeking employment elsewhere, they devoted their time to their farms, because they found they could not only make a good living but profits besides.

The colonization project in Silverhill is unique when we compare it with similar undertakings in various parts of the country. It is common for the colonizers (after a community has been settled or the land sold) to leave and let the settlers shift for themselves. The leader of the colonization company in Silverhill, Mr. Oscar Johnson, departed from that policy and remained in Silverhill, participating in the activities of the settlers and sharing the disappointments. He has always been found in the lead and has always considered as of first importance the welfare of the people in the community. It is natural that, in pioneering, all have to do their part, and if we should endeavor to set down what part each and every one has played it would indeed be a long history. We feel that Mr. Johnson has so well represented, in every particular, the aspirations of the settlers that hardly any other need be mentioned. This is particularly true because he has always enjoyed the confidence of his fellowmen, both within and without the community.

In 1905 Mr. and Mrs. Winberg moved to Silverhill from Chicago, Illinois, and Mr. Winberg, being particularly interested in scientific agriculture and co-operation, began in 1906 to interest the people in the former and proceeded to show also the benefits to be derived from co-operative selling and buying. We believe that this has added, in some degree, to the progressive development of agriculture in Baldwin County. In 1910 Mr. Winberg started the Satsuma orange development on a commercial scale, and has, since that time, devoted his energies toward the development of that branch of horticulture throughout the Gulf Coast section.

In 1904 Mr. A. A. Norden and family moved to Silverhill from Omaha, Nebraska, and established a hotel, which has ever since been known as the Hotel Norden, and is now, since the death of Mr. Norden, maintained by Mrs. Norden and her daughter, Mrs. Anderson. A hotel, when well conducted, is a most valuable asset to a community, and this particular hotel has been that to the fullest extent, because of the splendid way in which it has been maintained—always with the view of making it pleasant for guests.

One of the early pioneers who added materially to the progress of Silverhill is Theodore A. Johnson, who established the first general store in this part of Baldwin County. In the early days his store did not only serve the people in the community but a wide adjacent territory. He is known as one of the best merchants in his line in the county, and the aid he has extended to the settlers in the community, particularly during the hard years in the early period, cannot be told, because, like Oscar Johnson, he does not mention the good he does.

In 1909, thirteen Bohemian families moved to Silverhill, thus starting the nucleus of a Bohemian settlement southwest of Silverhill. This small number has since grown to something like seventy-five families in the Silverhill district, all of whom have proven themselves not only good farmers but splendid citizens and have done their share in the development of the district and aided in the prosperity of the entire community.

In 1926 the village of Silverhill was incorporated, with Oscar Johnson as its mayor. The town now has three churches, a school, two general stores, one bank and other businesses. The population within the corporate limits is 300, but the population in the Silverhill district numbers over 400 families, with the town of Silverhill as the community center.

GERMANS AT ELBERTA

(By L. Lindoerfer)

Elberta was founded by the Baldwin County Colonization Company in 1905. Henry C. Bartling was secretary and manager of the company. The property secured consisted of 53,000 acres, contracted from the Southern States Lumber Company. The first thing the Baldwin County Colonization Company did was to build roads on every section line, also every half mile running east and west, so that every forty-acre tract would be on a road. One-room school houses were built every two to four miles.

In colonizing the section a number of stumbling-blocks were encountered—storms, yellow fever, etc. The Elberta district is settled mostly by Germans, who during the war not only purchased their quota of Liberty bonds but willingly sent their boys over the sea.

Elberta has a consolidated school doing Junior High School work. The children at a distance are brought in on trucks, three trucks being needed, and one truck takes the Senior High School pupils on to Foley—to the High School there. Besides the Public School there are two parochial schools—Catholic and Lutheran. As the Lutherans have no teacher at present for this section, they are attending the Public School. Elberta has four churches: Catholic, Ohio Lutheran, Missouri Lutheran, and Christian Alliance. It is a thriving little town, with four general stores, one hardware store, one meat market, a bank, and a hotel. There are between four and five hundred families in the Elberta district. The farmers are doing well, and have well built homes and barns. West of Elberta, five and one-half miles, is Foley, the shipping point, while Miflin on Wolf's Bay is only three and one-half miles south, with a fine bathing beach.

POLISH COLONY

The first Polish settlers were brought here by the Southern Development Lumber Company in 1906. There were forty-three families the first year, and two families direct from the old country soon followed. The Poles have a Catholic church in Summerdale, but there are only seven families left, all farmers, scattered about in other communities.

GREEK COLONY

The Greek colony is the only "communistic" group in the county, all members living in a large, attractive house on the "Plantation." Many Greeks upon arriving in this country are sheltered here from the exploiter until they have learned its language and customs.

"Mr. J. Malbis," it is recorded, "came to the United States in 1906 for a visit of two or three months, on a vacation. His main object in spending his vacation here was to see what the United States really was. He traveled throughout thirty-six states of the Union in ninety days— and was ready to return to Europe the next week. However, after thinking over the matter, he decided to remain here for life."

Mr. Malbis himself says: "From all that I had heard about the country and its opportunities, I gathered that the South was the poorest part in every way—soil, products, money, etc. For this reason I decided from force of duty to select a section thereof and work to improve it. I arrived in Mobile, and purchased my first piece of land a few days after my arrival. The transaction was completed January 17, 1907, for two sections of land in Baldwin County. One of these is the present site of my large Plantation.

"Our object is to equip this part of the county that I own with good roads, beautiful parks, electric power, running water, an ice plant, a canning factory, etc.; in other words, to make it as nearly perfect as possible. Then any one who will prove that he is interested in farming and improving the land can purchase as much as he requires at cost price. My only requirement is that he must be a help and a credit to Baldwin County— to improve and advance the county at every opportunity. Our outside interests are for the betterment of the town or city they are in; for we Greeks try to progress in every way as we have the opportunity. My own entire work is not for money, but for creation."

BOHEMIAN COLONY

(From data furnished by A. F. Wesley and A. J. Cejka)

The reason for the emigration of the Bohemians from their home country is the love of liberty, but we must go far back into their history to substantiate this. The first emigrant to America was Augustine Herman—by way of Dutch-port in 1660. He founded in 1663 Bohemia Manor in Maryland, on 20,000 acres of land granted to him in recognition of services in drawing the maps of Virginia and Maryland.

Emigration from the year 1848 progressed very slowly on account of prohibitive regulations of the government. The majority of the emigrants were artisans inclined to agriculture. They settled mostly in Wisconsin, then spread to Iowa and Nebraska, and today you can meet them in every state of the Union.

The local Bohemian Colony has perhaps the most remarkable record of any in the county. Comparing the period of twenty years from its birth in 1908 to the present time, and considering the excellent progress made in agriculture and in social life, every impartial observer must give credit to those Bohemian toilers whose tools not only yielded a blessing to their families but contributed considerably to the wealth of this county, and indeed to that of the State of Alabama.

The origin of the Bohemian Colony is to be credited to Mr. Oscar Johnson of Silverhill. In 1908 Mr. Johnson advertised for a diligent land agent capable of colonizing the environs of Silverhill, Robertsdale and Summerdale. His advertisement was answered by Mr. Karal Hanak, of Texas, who finally decided to accept Mr. Johnson's liberal offer and to move to Silverhill. Mr. Hanak was well educated and came from a very prominent family in Moravia, now a part of Czecho-Slovakia. His plans were soon made for founding a Bohemian town like one in his native country bearing the name "Cechie." This plan failed from lack of knowledge of American farming, for one real American farmer requires more ground for his production than the people of a whole town in Hanak's native country. However, through his efforts the spark animated by a handful of painstaking and persistent settlers blazed up to one of the greatest successes.

The first pioneer of the colony, Mr. Joseph Kulieka, from Texas, arrived at Silverhill with his family in October, 1909, and is still living there. From 1909 to 1911 many others came to make their homes in Silverhill, but, becoming discouraged after a few years of hard work and unavoidable reverses, Mr. Hanak abandoned the project and left Silverhill in 1912. Others, however, continued his work so well begun, and additions to the colony became more and more numerous—one hundred and eight families at one time being located in twenty-two months—until they now number about two hundred and fifty families (over one thousand persons), and some individuals are prosperous merchants and mechanics as well as farmers. All have new modern homes, comfortably furnished, in place of the shanties that were the joint shelter for human beings and live stock in the past. One million dollars is probably not an overestimate of the property values they now hold.

The Bohemians are industrious, law-abiding people, and their ambition is to build up the country, to broaden the intelligence of their members by means of instructive lectures and other entertainment, and to lead them to enlightenment. Especially bearing in mind their immigrant countrymen, and seeking to aid them to become upright American citizens, an Instructive and Amusing Club was formed, also a Singing Society, "Bedrich Smetana," with its ladies' branch, "Libuse." They have organized in addition two very popular bands. To accommodate and encourage these social activities, two Community Halls have been built—one in Silverhill and the other in Robertsdale. Two fraternal lodges have been formed, which not only protect the families in case of sickness or death but have done much to foster unity among the members and promote the expansion of the colony. To improve marketing conditions two farmers' associations were formed: The Independent Growers and Shippers Association and the Hub Truckers Association, both of which have been of great service.

The colonists have settled around Robertsdale, Summerdale and in the Sonora district as well as Silverhill, and are most prosperous, depending entirely upon agricultural and horticultural resources.

FRENCH COLONY

(By Carl Boseck)

By a strange irony of fate, so often occurring in history, the descendant of Duchesneau, the French intendant, implacable foe of the great La Salle, generations later crossed and recrossed the paths blazed by this intrepid hero who died in the wilds of Texas at the hands of disaffected followers. Something of the spirit of his forebear coursed in the blood of F. X. Duchesneau, born in Montreal, of which his father also was a native, in 1843, but in early youth striking out for adventure and conquest, first in Ontario, next in the Dakotas, then in Nevada, and last in Baldwin County, Alabama.

Seeking health for his ailing wife, who had shared with him the rigors of pioneer life, he left the frozen prairies of North Dakota along the Canadian border in 1909 and came to Fairhope. But it was too late for her, who was taken back north to die. However, climate and sunshine had rejuvenated Mr. Duchesneau even in the short time he had been in Fairhope, and shortly after he came down again to learn for himself whether at his age under Baldwin County skies the soil would give him sustenance. In the interim, fellow-Canadian Frenchmen had been persuaded to give up their precarious living in North Dakota and in the Province of Saskatchewan and exchange it for the possibilities of Baldwin County.

In 1911 Gregory Ecoeur, a life-time friend of Mr. Duchesneau, under whom he had learned farming, had come into what is now the Elsanor district and had erected the first two-story house east of Robertsdale, then a hamlet of fewer than a dozen buildings. He had been dairying in the State of Washington and expected to do likewise here; but, when he found no market for the products of the cow, he settled down to general farming. He was followed by Adelor Riendeau, a former storekeeper, who erected a house within sight of that of Mr. Ecoeur's and who also went to farming. He found the soil responsive; but Pensacola was the only and at best a precarious market for his produce, which he took in a small wagon weekly to that city, involving then a rough trip of three and often more days.

Mr. Duchesneau, reluctant to invest in land until after personal experience in farming, arranged to clear and plant part of a son-in-law's holdings. Southern methods were different from what he had been accustomed to, but with the aid of Messrs. Ecoeur and Riendeau he soon learned to adapt himself to his new environment. The adventure put new life into him, so that before long he outdid those of younger years, and when his son-in-law Ulderic Riendeau came to take possession of his place he found a comfortable home and cleared acreage large enough to keep his family. Then nearing his eightieth birthday, Mr. Duchesneau, satisfied that work here as elsewhere made for success, bought and began to subdue a piece of land. He built another home and large barns, set out orchards and groves, and planted ornamental trees, shrubbery and flowers, putting to shame many younger men. And when fire destroyed his home he refused to live with children or friends but built anew, more substantially and better than before, demonstrating his faith in his adopted country.

Ardent churchmen, these Canadian French early sought out the ministrations of their religion, and Father Thomas came monthly from Elberta to give them the solace they had been taught to look for. When he suggested that a chapel be erected as more appropriate for divine service than an improvised altar in a private home, Ulderic Riendeau donated needed land on an eminence overlooking the Old Spanish Trail, now known as United States Highway No. 90, and every man in the colony aided in the erection of what is one of the finest small chapels of the Roman Church on the Gulf Coast. Free of all encumbrances, it was consecrated by the late Bishop Allen, neighbors of all creeds joining in the auspicious services. The first child to be baptized in the chapel was that of Mr. and Mrs. Eugene Cosavent, while the first grave in the adjoining churchyard is occupied by the remains of the late Ulderic Riendeau, former owner of the plot.

Industry, thrift, and interest in education and the church are the dominating traits that characterize these French people, who preserve in their community the language and many of the customs that still make their Quebec provincial home a little France in America.

CROATIANS AT DYAS
(By Mrs. Blaz Grdjan)

The Croatians, or Jugoslavs, began to settle in Baldwin County about the year 1913. The majority of these people came to the United States in the early 1900's or before and settled in the states of Illinois, Missouri, Iowa, Colorado and Wisconsin. Their occupation in the above states was mostly mining; but, becoming tired of such hazardous work, some decided to try farming, which, if not yielding a large profit, at least afforded them a better and healthier life.

The first few years were very hard, as the majority bought woodland and had to clear the ground of stumps and trees before they could begin plowing. The farmers' unions were poorly organized and the crops sometimes could not be sold, and even if marketed the return was only about one-third of what had been spent for seed and fertilizer. About 1922, however, markets had begun to expand and improve. Now we raise Irish and sweet potatoes, cabbage, and cotton; also plant home gardens. The Farmers' Co-operative Union of Perdido ships and sells all our produce with the right kind of organization. We are more prosperous, and many are building beautiful homes, which, with the sale of vegetables, dairy cows and poultry, we are paying for.

There are about 11 Jugoslav families in this colony, some farms adjoining and some scattered to a distance of about one to three miles apart. There are several in Silverhill also. The Jugoslav farmers in Perdido and Dyas have an average of forty acres of land per family. The children attend the Perdido school, to which they are conveyed by bus. The Jugoslav people are mostly Catholics, but they have no church of their own here.

AMISH COLONY

(Data furnished by A. N. Schrock)

This is a religious colony sometimes called the Hooker Mennonites because they use hooks and eyes instead of buttons on their clothes. Originally living in Kansas, those now resident in Baldwin County belonged to a church called Amish Mennonites, but "they at all would not live up to Scripture, and there were a few living in Arizona who seemed in general of one mind and one accord with us—therefore moved here."

They left Arizona early in 1917 on account of dissatisfaction with the schools, and they chose Baldwin County on account of its warm climate and cheap lands. There are five families and twenty-two members in all. They own six hundred and sixty acres near Bay Minette, and are engaged in farming, poultry raising, dairying and turpentine. They have a house of worship, a good school and seem well satisfied. Although born in this country, they are of German descent.

"Our interest is in the Almighty Father, a perfect God and His Holy Word. Awaiting a home in Heaven, yours, etc."

Doubtless many other nationalities may be found in the county, but so far as can be ascertained they are in no sense organized in communities or colonies.

Towns of importance from other viewpoints are mentioned in our concluding section:

MODERN BALDWIN

Alabama, as outlined on our maps, is shaped like a short-handled cleaver. The handle is bisected by Mobile Bay, and the eastern half of it and that part of the state extending farthest south is Baldwin County. With the exception of seventeen miles in the extreme northeast bordering Escambia County, it is entirely surrounded by water, having Little River on the north, the Tombigbee, Alabama, Apalachee and Tensaw Rivers forming the northern part of the western boundary, Perdido River on the east, and approximately six hundred miles of shore line, bordered on the lower western side by Mobile Bay and its many tributary inlets, and on the south and east by the Gulf of Mexico and Perdido Bay.

The county is approximately 72 miles long by 32 miles wide, and contains in its area of 1,585 square miles scenery diversified and picturesque. Across the northern half the foot-hills of the great Appalachian system wear themselves out in rolling uplands until they reach Mobile Bay, creating at that point Sea Cliff, the highest spot on tide-water between New Jersey and the coast of southern Texas. The southern half is a coastal plain descending gradually to the Gulf. Bay Minette, the county seat, in the central part of Baldwin, claims an elevation of 268 feet, while Foley in the southern part is estimated to be 80 feet above sea-level.

Situated in what is known as the equable zone, there are no extremes of temperature. In this peninsular county the climate is tempered by moisture from many surrounding waters and a copious annual rainfall of approximately 63 inches. The mean temperature for the summer months is 81°, and the warmest days are made delightful by the fresh breezes from the Gulf. The freezing point is seldom reached during the winter, and that season approaches the ideal in weather crisp enough to be stimulating, with balmy days of brilliant sunshine when fires and wraps are not needed.

The entire country is of surpassing beauty and offers a great variety of scenic growth to the lover of nature. There are thousands of acres of primeval pine and oak forests, and all flora indigenous to the temperate and semi-tropical regions flourish here. Among other trees, the poplar, cedar, sweet gum and magnolia thrive. In the spring the woods are a riot of dog-wood blossom and yellow jessamine, and in the winter are brightened by holly and gay yupon. The picture is always colorful, especially in the ravines of Fairhope and other parts of the county where the soft-toned red clay banks and roads lend relief to the varied hues of the foliage. The northern section of picturesque wooded hills and valleys, the western shore-line of tree-crowned cliffs descending in the south to the low palmetto-bordered shores of the lagoons and rivers, shadowed by giant moss-hung oaks, the pine-covered plains of the central and southern region—all have their own peculiar charm. World travelers assert that the scenery along the crystal-clear waters of South Baldwin, part of the lately designated American Riviera, is not excelled even by the beauties of the far-famed Mediterranean shore.

It is probable that Baldwin County is surrounded by and contains within its boundaries a greater mileage of navigable waters than any other county in the country. Its streams, notably Perdido, Fish, Magnolia and Bon Secour Rivers, which penetrate it in the south, as well as the lakes near-by, offer to the angler almost every species of fish to be caught in fresh water—such as black bass, bream, goggle eye, perch and white fish, while almost every variety of salt-water fish to be caught in the Gulf abounds in the many bays and lagoons. Among others are the pompano, Spanish mackerel, sheepshead, red fish, tarpon and cavalho. Shrimp and crabs are plentiful, and from the shallow waters of the bays are taken some of the finest oysters in the world, there being a universal demand for the Bon Secour "Plants."

The fields and marshes abound in game such as ducks, quail and dove, while wild turkey, bear and deer to be found in other sections make the entire county the sportsman's "happy hunting-ground." The bird-lover pursues his game with other purposes, and finds delight in the mocking bird, the lark, the brilliant cardinal and flicker and many other natives, as well as various kinds of migratory birds that flash through the woods.

Until long after the War between the States, Baldwin County was held in vast estates, according to the custom of the South. It was not until men of vision, realizing the potential wealth of the section through intensified and diversified farming, made small acreages available that the era of great development began. In this they were pioneers. It is still altogether a rural county, the largest town, Bay Minette, founded by J. D. Hand, and incorporated in 1908, having a population of only 2,000. Other towns incorporated since then are Foley, founded by John B. Foley, with an estimated population of 800; Fairhope, claiming 1,500; Robertsdale, with a population of 450; Silverhill, having 225 residents, and very recently Daphne, with a citizenship of 200. Each of these communities is the trading center for many thousands of people from the adjacent farms. In all of them are found attractive modern homes and in most of them electric light and ice plants, water and sewerage systems, bakeries, laundries and all improvements conducive to comfortable living. Telephone lines and the R. F. D. system reach the farthest limits of the county, mail being delivered to the hamlets along the southern rivers and bays by launch.

The census of 1920 gave Baldwin a population of 20,734; twenty-five thousand is a conservative estimate of the present population. It is safe to say that this is comprised of the most cosmopolitan citizenship assembled in any rural section of the south. All quarters of the United States are represented, and almost every nationality, the foreign colonizing companies having devoted themselves to bringing in people from their own countries.

The progress of the county agriculturally is largely due to the perseverance, industry and thrift of these people. In 1921 the total tax was $208,512.88, divided as follows; state, $75,296.31; county, $133,216.56. In 1927 the state tax was $106,108.79; county tax, $187,730.94—a total of $293,839.73.

As it is true that banks are the "pulse" of the communities they serve, the following figures are given indicating the growth of the eight monetary institutions in the county. The Baldwin County Bank, Bay Minette, was the first to organize, being established in 1902 with resources of $15,000; present resources are $1,060,148.96. The Robertsdale Bank, organized in 1911 (with resources of $40,000 in 1917), estimates its present resources at $438,850.17. The Bank of Fairhope opened its doors in 1917, claiming resources of $16,561.21. Its present resources total $380,435.68. The Bank of Daphne was established in 1920, with resources of $30,000.00. It claims present resources of $100,000.00. The Bank of Loxley began business in 1920 with resources of $25,996.21; its present resources are $204,000. The Bank of Silverhill, which opened in 1924, at present is capitalized at $20,000. The State Bank of Foley and the South Baldwin State Bank were merged January 1st, 1925, becoming the Farmers and Merchants Bank, with total resources of $430,000; present resources are $560,000.

The progress of a territory is in direct ratio to its transportation facilities, and the people of Baldwin County have insured a future of unprecedented prosperity in the program of road-building already under way. In the near future $850,000 will be spent in improving and building roads, and a small paving project is already in view. The opening of the great Cochrane Bridge across Mobile Bay in June, 1927, affords rapid transportation to Mobile by auto, and is an important link in the historic Old Spanish Trail which crosses the county to that other thriving city, Pensacola, Florida. The Over-state Transit Company has recently inaugurated a double daily bus service between the two cities, and also serves the towns of the Eastern Shore and central and southern sections. Direct mail service is maintained in this way. State highways cross the county in all directions.

The main line of the L. and N. Railroad bisects Baldwin, affording prompt and direct transportation for freight and passengers. In 1905 the Bay Minette and Fort Morgan Line was built to penetrate the center of the county directly south of the county seat as far as Foley, and probably no other single venture has contributed so much to the development of this territory. To this is due the phenomenal growth of South Baldwin, and this is rated one of the most profitable branches of this great railroad system. Lying adjacent to Mobile, Baldwin County benefits by the excellent train service that unites that city of over 60,000 people with every part of the country as well as by the shipping facilities of that flourishing seaport and Pensacola. The recently inaugurated twenty-two and one-half hour train from Chicago to Mobile makes this Riviera section quickly accessible from points north and east.

For generations direct communication between Mobile and the Eastern Shore has been maintained by boats giving passenger and freight service, and of late years providing space for automobiles. The charm and beauty of the trip across Mobile Bay will secure for this service sufficient patronage to assure its continuance. Small packets also make regular trips to Bon Secour and Fish River points.

It is impossible to think of Alabama without visioning cotton fields, but this section produces less cotton than any other portion of the state. The thousands of acres of yellow pine forests have made it primarily a lumbering country, and from that industry has sprung the establishment of many sawmills and plants engaged in the production of turpentine and naval stores. As an outgrowth of this industry may also be noted a veneer mill, sash and door, and hamper, crate and box factories.

The present great development of the commonwealth is due to the utilization of cut-over land in the cultivation of the satsuma orange and pecan, the creation of truck farms, and progress in the raising of live stock and poultry. Although there are many varieties of soil throughout the length and breadth of Baldwin, it is for the most part sandy loam with clay sub-soil. It is easily worked; it responds generously to intelligent tillage, and, quickened by an abundant rainfall, has made the county a leader in agricultural production. This is the situation—when less than 10% of the total area is under cultivation.

The distinctive product of South Baldwin is the satsuma crop, this fruit thriving only in the coastal region. The industry has struggled through a period of experimentation, but is now on a firm basis, and the Gulf Coast Citrus Exchange has found a national market for this luscious seedless orange. It is estimated that not more than 3,500 acres are planted in satsumas, but the returns from this year's crop are appraised at $100,000. Another product for which the county is famous is the pecan. Through selection and grafting, many fine paper-shell varieties of this nut have been evolved that flourish in this soil, and the thousands of pounds of nuts marketed annually bring in a large revenue.

Throughout the county are truck farms producing remarkable returns for the time and money invested. The mild climate making all-year cultivation possible, in many cases the production of two or three crops, the splendid marketing facilities by rail, boat and highway, have been the chief factors in the development of this enterprise. Baldwin County leads the state in the output of sweet and Irish potatoes; and other crops such as cabbage, cucumbers, onions, sweet corn and melons brought the total value of produce shipped last season to $2,250,000. Every variety of vegetable can be grown successfully. The peanut crop is also profitable, and the soil is well adapted to the production of sugar-cane. Some of the most delicious watermelons grown are produced in the county, notably in the Bon Secour section, and are shipped to all points of the compass.

Many fruits and berries thrive and are a source of income, among them being figs, pears, persimmons, plums, blackberries and dewberries, which are native, and strawberries, as well as several varieties of grapes.

Tobacco-growing, which began as an experiment in 1918, is now a profitable industry, although its cultivation is confined mainly to the plantation of sixty-five acres, all under shade, situated at Summerdale and owned by the Alabama Tobacco Growing Corporation. This product is of the Sumatra type used principally for cigar wrappers, and a ready market is found for the entire output as soon as it is packed. The production for this year will approximate five hundred bales, weighing one hundred and thirty-five pounds each.

At the Greek settlement of Mr. Malbis it has been found that olive trees may be grown with success, and the culture of silk-worms has been tried far enough to assure a future for this industry. Here also is operated a canning factory, which is supplied by the fruit and vegetables grown in the vicinity.

All-year grazing conditions, the adaptability of the soil to forage crops, and the presence of countless creeks and springs produce an ideal country for stock-raising and dairying. Recently many car-loads of cows, hogs and sheep were shipped, which augurs well for the future of this infant industry. Great progress has been made in dairying, and the products are utilized by five creameries, which cannot supply the demand for their output. Poultry-raising also is coming to the front as a profitable occupation, and shipments of chickens and eggs are heavy, while Baldwin County hatcheries supply a wide area.

Satsuma nurseries have flourished since the beginning of the industry, but of late years florists have found the soil and climate adaptable to their needs, and in the southern part of the county are to be found several expensive enterprises of this nature. From green-houses, acres of roses, canna and other flowers and a variety of shrubs the nurserymen ship to all sections of the country.

Hence it would appear that there is no branch of agriculture that may not be pursued with profit and with less effort than in many other sections. When one considers the fact that Baldwin County is fast taking the lead in the state in the production of farm products, and that such astonishing returns are produced from the cultivation of so small an acreage in a sparsely-settled county, it would seem that development has only just begun.

It is to be presumed that there are great undeveloped resources, as geologists claim—stating, for instance, that in this section are to be found the richest potential oil-fields in the country. There are exhaustless deposits of tile, porcelain and building clays. The pottery at Daphne for many years has been engaged in the manufacture of useful and ornamental products, while the Art Department of the School of Organic

Education, Fairhope, creates many articles of great beauty from the various clays. At Clay City, on Fish River, is found one of the greatest deposits south of the Ohio River, the variety ranging from pottery to the finest brick clays. A kiln established there produces bricks and building and drainage tiles. Long before the War between the States this clay was shipped to New Orleans, where it was used in potteries and in the manufacture of brick.

While Baldwin County has been forging ahead agriculturally and commercially, the cultural and religious side of life has been in no way neglected. Throughout the county are to be found churches of the Baptist, Methodist, Presbyterian, Episcopal and Roman Catholic denominations, and in some sections Lutheran and Christian. The Christian Scientists and Theosophists are also represented, and Fairhope claims to have among its residents adherents of twenty-six distinct sects and cults.

The development of educational facilities is in keeping with the progress in other directions, and the county is entering upon an era of school improvement that will provide for the constantly increasing demands. Well-equipped grade and high schools are maintained in all sections of the county, and the system culminates in a state normal at Daphne. The internationally known School of Organic Education at Fairhope, a boarding and day school established by Marietta Johnson assisted by Mr. and Mrs. S. H. Comings, attracts many visitors annually to that growing center. There is also a private school in Elberta under the direction of the Catholic priests. Adequate negro schools are established by the county, and there is a Normal and Industrial School for the colored race at Daphne.

Five public libraries in the county administer to the intellectual needs of both old and young. The Fairhope Library, established in 1911, has a commodious building housing nearly 10,000 volumes. The Point Clear Library of 1,434 volumes, established in 1921, also occupies its own building. The institution at Robertsdale was opened in 1914 and now has on its shelves 1,500 books. The Bay Minette Public Library, dating from 1922, has 2,700 volumes, while the Foley Library, housed in its own building, contains 2,000 volumes. All of the larger towns have well-equipped moving picture theatres, which provide entertainment with well selected programs.

Among the county's greatest assets may be listed the four newspapers published weekly, which efficiently maintain the publicity so necessary to the onward and upward march of any community. The "Baldwin Times" of Bay Minette, owned and edited by R. B. Vail; "The Onlooker," Foley, owned and edited by the Barchards; the "Courier," Fairhope, primarily a single tax paper, edited by the owner, E. B. Gaston; and the "Baldwin County News," Foley, at present owned by C. M. Balzli, Jr., but having as its presiding genius through many vicissitudes that newspaper woman of outstanding ability, Mrs. John

Stark—all carry to subscribers in every section of the Union their message of faith and progress.

In the towns throughout the county flourish the usual fraternal organizations, Chambers of Commerce, Parent-Teachers Associations and many excellent women's clubs, both cultural and civic. These latter are united in a large and active County Council of Federated Clubs. There is a strong County League of Women Voters and an active Tuberculosis Association of county scope, and the lovers of Baldwin legend and history are drawn together in the Baldwin County Historical Society.

Since 1912 the county has maintained a Home Demonstration Agent, and much excellent work has been done among girls' and women's clubs by giving practical instruction in poultry raising and gardening as well as teaching the members to can, preserve, sew and make hats, and acquainting them with all other phases of home economics.

Baldwin was among the first counties in Alabama to engage an all-time Health Officer. The Health Unit was established in 1921, and the personnel in addition to the physician in charge consists of a trained nurse and a sanitary inspector. General supervision is exercised over all matters pertaining to the prevention of disease, a large part of the work being educational. Some of the most important activities are: the examination annually of school children and the correction of defects found; the giving of vaccines and inoculation for the prevention of small-pox, typhoid and diphtheria; maternity and infancy welfare work; control of sanitation and supervision of water supplies and the inspection of hotels and food-handling places.

The hotels of the county are unexcelled, being far superior to those usually found in towns of similar size. They are above the average in standards of comfort and cuisine, and cater to an exclusive clientele. Among the best are the Trammel Hotel at Bay Minette; the Colonial Inn (overlooking Mobile Bay) and the commodious Fairhope Hotel, both at Fairhope; and the new $200,000 hostelry at Foley. Contracts have been let for a splendid new hotel at Bay Minette, to be known as the New Trammel. The capacity of these establishments is frequently taxed, for Baldwin County is famed far and wide as an ideal winter and summer resort. The excellent golf courses maintained by the Country Clubs in many towns are a great attraction to lovers of the game.

Hundreds of miles of shore-line offer to the sportsman boating and swimming in the tranquil waters of many bays or the surf of the Gulf, as well as hunting and fishing not to be surpassed anywhere in the country. On the Eastern Shore of Mobile Bay the Point Clear Hotel, open in summer, and the Beach Hotel, Battles, which extends its hospitality to guests throughout the year, attract a large patronage, and the view of water and sky from these places is superb. Magnolia Springs, on Magnolia River, in the heart of the Riviera country, and the site of the exclusive Governor's Club, is also an ideal resort. A spacious new hotel at Perdido Beach and another at Lillian add to the charm of these two hamlets, which lie in verdant beauty along the blue waters of Perdido Bay. On the Gulf Coast the vast stretch of snow-white sand and safe beach present features unexcelled by the most famous places of the kind. Recently the Gulf Shores Development Company established a pavilion there, which is a forecast of the possibilities of the section.

This commonwealth has frequently been called the "Empire of Baldwin," and when its many advantages are considered it seems to be justly named. Nowhere has Nature been more bountiful in gifts of location, beauty, climate and fertility. With its thousands of acres still covered with virginal forests, and with the amazing chronicled results produced from the cultivation of so small a percentage of its total area, it is true that the development of the county has only begun, and that with the inauguration of a stupendous road building program, with a cosmopolitan citizenship of far-sighted and enterprising men and women, it is impossible for the most sanguine to vision the inevitably great attainments of the future. It is a far cry from the mud-plastered huts of the aborigines to the modern towns of the present, and from Indian trails to improved modern highways; but the achievements lying ahead will be in even greater proportion, and those fortunate enough to live here will find themselves participants in that greatest of all romances—the evolution of a country.

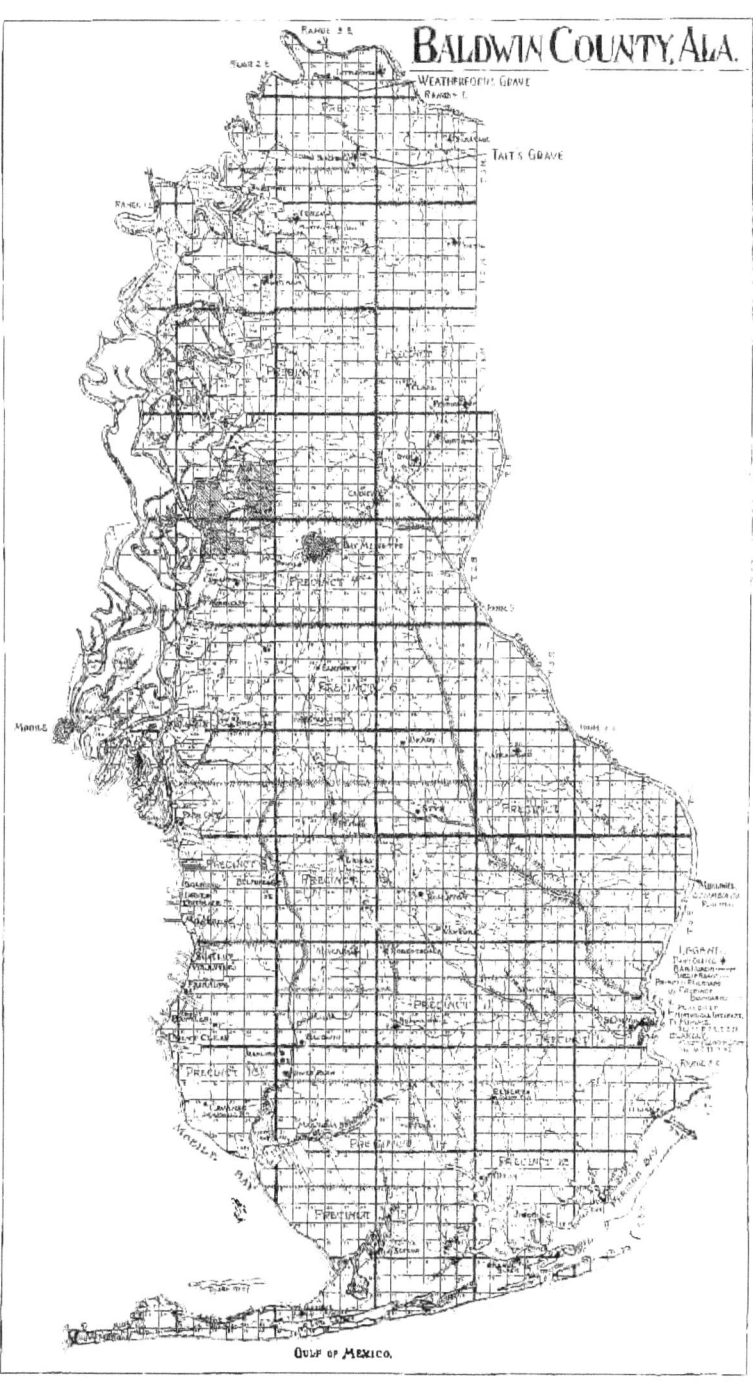

www.ingramcontent.com/pod-product-compliance
Lightning Source LLC
Chambersburg PA
CBHW070517090426
42735CB00012B/2813